I0116397

Across the Crooked Bridge

Growing up in North Idaho and the Silver Valley

Eloise Kraemer

Haumea Publishing Co.

ACROSS THE CROOKED BRIDGE

Haumea Publishing Co.

First Edition

Printed by CreateSpace, Charleston, S.C., USA

ISBN: 978-0-692-41781-8

Dedication

This book is dedicated to my grandchildren, grand nieces, and grand nephews in the hope that they, and all children of the world, will continue to explore and seek out their own magical forest path that will help them to learn, grow, and foster imagination, ingenuity and invention.

The cicatrices of enlightenment create the contours of our soul.

EeKraemer

Table of Contents

Table of Contents Continued

Introduction

The Crooked Bridge

The bridge was not always crooked. She got that way over the years. She rested on top of railroad ties that were stacked as a box and set into each bank filled with rock. Her mid section sat on two very large steam boilers, recycled from old mills. They had their tops cut out and were filled huge boulders, then set in the bed of the river. She was dressed in an assortment of planks, telephone poles and railroad ties, and crossed a sixty foot span of the then muddy gray South Fork of the Coeur d'Alene River. She was built by my father in 1953 and torn down by the construction of Interstate 90 in about 1976.

Today, children have personal computers, laptops, 'iPods', 'iPads', 'Kindles' and other internet connected devices too numerous to mention. Our world has become more interconnected through twenty-four hour world news broadcasts, interstate freeways, international airports, world-wide internet access, 'GPS', and smart phones.

Fifty years ago, as a child, my access to the rest of the world was by way of a wooden bridge. The bridge set my family apart from the world to a certain extent, like an island. It had a mountain and "enchanted" forest for the backdrop. The foreground was a gray river that shone silver in the moonlight and hid untold treasures.

I grew up in a family of nine, with two brothers and four sisters. As children, we were forbidden to go across the bridge unless we were on our way to school or with our parents, until we were teenagers. Even as teenagers, we needed permission to cross the bridge, and access was granted on a case by case basis. We always looked forward to the start of school in the fall when our world opened up.

Rules were made to be broken. I can't say we abided by our parent's rules on all occasions. There was "backdoor" access on the west side of our home by way of an ancient roadbed. This roadbed was the old state highway that originally ran along the north side of the mountain to the east and into Wallace. We used the old roadbed to come and go to our home on the west side, before the bridge was built. When I was about four years old, my father built the bridge on the east side of our place. After the bridge was built, the old roadbed caved in and was no longer navigable by car. We could still walk this route, to the west, to a neighborhood store, if the need arose. Sometimes we got permission to do this. Other times, my siblings and I sneaked around to the other side of the hill just to see what was going on.

My brother and I sneaked out and over the bridge with our bikes sometimes when we were about eleven and thirteen years old. We would look for "junk" metal along the railroad tracks that went towards town. We eventually got caught by our mother. That was the last time we went. I got spanked pretty badly. My brother ran, but my father dealt with him later. That was the end of that.

Chapter 1 – The Cave

There it is again! I hear distant thunder rumbling, like a roller on an old washboard. Then, the rain hits. It hits heavy, in sheets, like someone washing the house with a hose. It washes over the roof, the siding, the windows, washing away the cobwebs of the past that have been gathering all night, stirred by the myriad of old photos that lay on the desk. Last night, I stayed up late, sorting pictures by date, putting names onto blurred faces – some, now ghosts of the past. Funny how time circles like a dog chasing its tail!

Here I lie in my sister's bed. Only minutes away from my family home where I slept in a similar bed so many years ago. The same sounds awake me; the chirping birds, scolding squirrels, a dog barking in the distance, and highway traffic in the valley. The traffic is made up, mostly, these days, of interstate commercial trucks and tourists passing through. Others are the locals, (storekeepers, laborers and miners) heading for the next day of working their way toward retirement. The tourists are usually on their way to some distant destination.

The rain slows to a trickle. The old dog, hateful of thunder, stirs from her bed in the corner and ventures out to test her breakfast, consisting of a neat little spread of kibbles and water on a mat, a bowl for each. To ensure her enjoyment of the meal, the kibbles are neatly colored like the corn cereal we would get sometimes in little sample packs when we were kids.

The rain has stopped now. The other dog sleeps still, on her back on the sofa. This is forbidden territory, not for the faint of heart, but, after all, her mistress has left her in the hands of a "marshmallow". She, being a dog of most mystical powers will make the most of this situation.

What child doesn't like to make the most of parents not being home? I became aware of this mystical dog's late evening wanderings the night before, and quietly covered the sofa with a sheet so we could both rest more easily, insuring that all will be well when the mistress returns. After all, you just don't mess with some things that don't need messing with!

As I stand watching the old dog's blissful sleep, I remember many circles of time ago, some children playing on a hot summer day. Thunder rumbled in the distance as the children readied themselves for an adventure into their secret hiding place. Their mother and father had left on a day trip into the big city of Spokane, Washington, about eighty miles away.

"We need a name for our secret club!"

"Well, what is it?"

"Our secret hiding place."

"Yeah, so what would we call it so that only we would know what we were talking about?"

"What about S. H. P.?" "That sounds like ship. I don't get it."

"No, think about it...S....H...P, Secret Hiding Place!"

"Oh, Yes!" The other two of us exclaimed in unison!" "That's really great!"

S. H. P., our secret hiding place, it had become.

We three "big kids" had formed our first real alliance – and tied it to the "little kids" (four more) making a band of seven of us, who, in unity and continuation throughout all the circles of time, had created our secret world, S. H .P..

What was it? It was an old mining tunnel that our parents had forbidden us to enter alone. The tunnel was in a hill behind our house. It had been originally created by an old miner back in the early 1900s. My parents dug it out and timbered it back several feet. The right fork was the smaller side, not timbered, and quickly slimmed down to just crawl space. You could probably only go about twelve feet in all. There were also bats back there. We agreed as a whole not to venture into that portion. Well, I do think I was back there a couple of times, once hiding from the world and once I crawled back there on a bet with my brother, (both were bad ideas).

The left side was vastly different. It broadened into a decent sized tunnel, and was timbered for about fourteen feet, almost to the end. The back four or five feet to the end of the tunnel, was clay and rock, mostly one huge rock at the end, so fairly stable. We added a few candles, some supplies (pre-packaged gelatin makes a great treat. Pour a little in your palm and lick the sweet mixture!) We stored water in Mason jars. We also stored saltine crackers and raisins in jars to keep the mice away. We kept apples from our old apple tree in an old tin box. Old wooden boxes were arranged for seats, tables and a storage cabinet. It held pencil and paper for ideas. We were all set!

We did break our code "Never Tell Anyone", just once. A power lineman came by, one day, hot, dusty, tired, and asked for a drink of water. Our parents had just left on a trip out to our grandmother's place on the north fork of the Coeur d'Alene River. That gave us about three quarters of the day to enjoy S.H.P.! It was a hot July day. The type of day you wished you had worn your shoes if you ventured off the lawn onto the old road bed that ran behind our house. The hard rocky surface was hot enough to fry an egg, and burned on the bottoms of our summer calloused feet. There was no wind and just enough moisture in the air from the river out front of the house to make the heat seem oppressive. The air was silent. All the song birds had escaped to the cool high mountain perches in the dense forest. The little rock squirrels that usually scampered to and fro forever gathering food to store for the winter, or more "stuffing" to line their nests were hiding underground in a semi deep slumber called 'aestivation', a summer-type hibernation. We were anxious, ourselves, to partake of the cool drafts that lay just beyond the entrance to the cave.

Here stood a sorrowful soul. He had been walking the power lines on the mountainside, looking for a problem. He was hot and thirsty. What to do? We all looked from one to the other and silently agreed to break our vow, just this once! We had quite an enjoyable visit with this lineman. He entertained us, and I'm sure we entertained him. I'm not sure who had more questions, us, about the electric lines and electricity, or him, about our life and our cave. We offered him some of our fare, consisting of raisins, graham crackers, water and apples. We told him we were sorry he hadn't brought along any of the power company's mules. The summer before, some men, working with the local power company, came through our place with about four pack mules. They were traveling along the power line that followed along the mountain behind our house. They were spraying the vegetation along the electric lines that ran above our home on the mountainside. They were all hot and tired when they stopped by our yard, asking for some water. We fed the mules apples and Mother filled her old wheelbarrow with water for the mules to drink. The men also enjoyed apples and fresh water from our spring. I still remember the pungent scent of the herbicide used to kill vegetation under the power lines. I can still smell the unfamiliar "horsey-muley" scent of the mules with their soft brown eyes and tall fuzzy ears. As huge and intimidating as they were, I remembering feeling compassion for them as we wiped off the soapy sweat that dripped off their enormous chests and from under their huge packs with thick harnesses. We watched them take in long draughts of the cool water while flicking pesky flies off their ominous heavily shod feet. After their short rest, the workers continued plodding off up over the rocky slope and up over the mountain, spraying vegetation as they went. We never saw them again after that summer day.

The lineman never did tell on us, sworn to secrecy as he was. He never reappeared to enjoy another day in the depths of our secret world, but he lived on in our hearts as a wandering white knight who stepped out of the forest one hot day.

We figured out how to make our own candles quite by accident. We had a problem soon on. We couldn't keep using the stubs of our mother's old candles without her becoming aware that something was amiss. We had forgotten some old color crayons out in the sun in the back yard near the entrance to the cave. My older sister was really angry when she discovered what we had done. Then....an idea formed. "What if – we could squish the already squishy colored wax around something that would burn like a wick? YES!" We could use Mother's old ball of string! We thenceforth, set out to save and pilfer old broken pieces of color crayon and wax, (paraffin off old jelly jars included, and any old pieces of string we saw). We would heat the old wax in the hot summer sun on the rocks inside old jar lids. We would then squish the wax into the appearance of candles with string laid in the middle of the squished log of wax. We had created colorful candles of incomparable and individual design! We stored these candles with our supplies in the back of the tunnel where they quickly cooled and lay ready for future use. Our way was lit! I wonder if I could go back into the tunnel today, if some of the ends of those candles still wait to shed flickering light and shadows on the damp walls. Unfortunately, over the more than fifty years since those days, the old cave timbers have become rotten and decayed and a portion of the mountain has caved over the entrance.

In the winter S.H.P. lay asleep under a thick blanket of snow that covered the entryway to our secret. In the spring S.H.P. was forbidden to all. Rocks would tumble, clay earth would slide and the cave would tremble with rock bursts from the constantly moving mountain. As the winter drew to a close each year, the warm winds of springtime melted winter snows. The earth would slowly warm from the golden sun above. The longer days of summer would signal that the time had come once again, to venture forth into S.H.P.. The secret of S.H.P. was kept like a precious treasure by the seven us, even as we left home one by one.

Years later, on a whim, while looking for the hiding place of a pesky raccoon, our mother stumbled upon our beloved crypt. I many times wonder, though, if our father ever knew, and sat back, as I do with the mystical dog, and just let things be. He might say that, "you just don't mess with some things that don't need messing with!"

Chapter 2 – A Convenient Playhouse

My father used to purchase old cars, no longer running and "strip" them of all marketable metals, or working parts, leaving just the empty body to be disposed of. In the "old days", prior to changes in laws, which started in the early 1970s, with the right equipment, a stripped car body could easily be used to shore up river banks. Our home had been an old dredge area for reclaiming lost minerals flushed down the river from milling in early mining days. A river, that was known to frequently overrun its bank in the springtime, passed through the southern border of our land. Some of these old stripped car bodies found a home on the edges of the broken down and washed over banks amongst the rocks, buried for eternity in a watery, rocky grave, making a great purchase for future tree roots that now line the banks. No worry about pollution. Every moveable part or storage place for gas or oil had already been removed from the metal skeleton prior to burial.

A couple of these metal skeletons, however, paused on the road to their demise. One ended up handily, gently placed under an old cedar tree on an old abandoned road bed above our home. It was conveniently located so that our mother might view activity through her kitchen window. A second one found a resting spot under some giant popular trees, just off the lawn and the other side of a large clothesline for hanging the family laundry, also in clear view of the kitchen window. Each was placed so as to be able to have its unique identity and small garden around it.

The dark blue car by the clothesline became my older sister, Lana's. Lana was the eldest child, being five years older than I. She made the dark blue car body into a store. She shared it with Dana, the fourth child in line. Dana was the middle child. She was too young to be a "big" kid, being almost four years younger than myself (the youngest of the "big" kids) and too old, by her standards, to be a "little kid". Dana was extremely articulate, a fact that both of my parents were proud of. They were also proud of my older sister, Lana's ability to be a solid helpmate, a good cook for her age. She was also considered very trustworthy with the babies. This was a handy thing, given that mother had her hands full with all of us. It was only natural that the two of them teamed up. My elder brother, Jimmy, was three years older than I, (Elle), the third child. We became known as the "troublemakers", when we divided into teams. My brother was fond of making his own rules. I was his loyal follower. I adored my older brother. We would spend hours fixing our house, the light blue skeleton, set snugly nestled under the old cedar tree. We would pretend that my brother "went to work" when he had to help my father on one project or another. I would take care of the dolls, doing the doll laundry and keeping a miniature garden of carrots, radishes and potatoes, or shopped at my sister's general store, when it was open. My sister, Lana, or just "Sissy", had short hours of play. Being Mother's primary helpmate, she had many daily duties such as baking, ironing, cleaning, taking care of the infants. I was second helpmate, but not regarded as trustworthy. I was considered a dreamer, and flighty, more inclined to fantasy and wild ideas, not steady and quiet like my elder sister of five years. From about ten years old, my duties included dusting, drying dishes, and folding laundry, keeping my room clean, feeding the chickens and entertaining two of the "little children". Those two "little children", consisted of my little brother, six years younger than I, Danny, and my little sister, Katie, eight years younger than I. I was not allowed the care of "the baby", my youngest sister, Natalie, who was under a year old. When I played house and had the two "little children" to entertain, they became "my children". I would fix meals of saltine crackers, radishes from the garden and wild blackberries with water from the spring. My father made a little sink of wood with a bread pan for the sink tub. We could wash our hands with little ivory soap bars, cut down from one large bar of ivory soap.

We furnished the old car with an old piece of carpet on the floor. Seats had been removed, as were the steering wheel and the pasted board divide between the seats and the trunk. An orange, brown and yellow, colorful old quilt served as the bed in the "bedroom" in the trunk area.

One day I was playing in the old car by myself, listening to the early evening chirping song of a robin. Mr. and Mrs. Robin had made their presence known for a time, and I had been thinking I would like to see where they lived. At that moment, she fluttered by the car window, intent upon getting back to her nest after a brief dinner outing. I set out to follow her stealthily. Up the mountain she went. I climbed after her, under bushes, scratching my face, crawling, at times, as quickly as I could, as the path steepened. I didn't have to go very far. There was the nest, mother robin ensconced upon her prize eggs. I proceeded to climb the old pine, aided by the fact that there was an embankment the tree grew out of, making the distance to a branch below the nest closer to the ground on that side. As I arrived at the nest, Mrs. Robin flew off in an angry flutter of wings and set to scolding me.

I paid no mind, intent upon my mission. There lay three beautiful blue robin eggs. Why, Mother Robin certainly wouldn't miss just one egg! I could hatch out and raise my very own robin baby! I quickly snatched the one egg and scuttled down the tree with Mother Robin screaming and dive bombing me all the way. Off I ran to my playhouse. I had a soft little purse in the playhouse. I figured this would be the perfect nest. I lined it with some old cotton stuffing that had fallen out of the old quilt we had lined the trunk of the car with. I gently tucked the egg into my handmade nest and squirreled it away in the "jockey box" of the old car body playhouse. The sun was setting in the western sky as I ran into our house, late for dinner.

Until full dark, as I was resting in my bed at night, I heard the robins' cries. My heart sank. I knew I had done the wrong thing. I awoke the next morning to the continued cries from the robins. I felt like a criminal, forever marked as an evil miscreant! No, I could fix things! I would show Mother and Father Robin that I could do just as good a job as them and lessen their load in the process! I pictured how happy they would be when I produced their child fully feathered and healthy, riding sublimely on my shoulder! Yes! I could do this! I sneaked out early in the morning to check the egg. It was cold! I thought the little wool purse and nice soft cotton, tucked away as it was in the jockey box would keep it warm. I didn't think about the fact that, once that warm summer sun sets, in northern Idaho, no matter how warm the day, the cooling effect of the forests and rivers begins to take effect, like a giant natural air conditioning system. The temperature in North Idaho where I lived usually ranged around 73 degrees in June during the sunny days, but could drop as low as 44 degrees on an average. I set to blowing on the egg and warming it with my hands. It slowly warmed. I tucked it back into its nest and ran back into the house. In the afternoon, I checked the egg. My goodness! The egg was really hot! The sun had spent the morning and early afternoon beating down on the hood of the old car skeleton. It had heated the surface up to the temperature of a warm griddle, thereby making the jockey box inside suffocating hot! I had not given a thought to this scenario. I had pictured my little egg in a fine little incubator safe from any harm. I moved the home made nest to the cupboard under my little sink, only to worry about it again being too cold later in the evening as the sun went down.

Needless to say, my little egg never did hatch. Eventually, I was encouraged by a most odorous smell, to quietly bury it under the old cedar tree and beg forgiveness from Mr. and Mrs. Robin, who, by then, were proudly displaying two beautiful, healthy, big mouthed offspring. I never interfered with nature heedlessly again.

Chapter 3 - Crooked Trees

I used to worry about one sided trees. When I was about nine years old, I asked my father why the evergreen trees on the hillside grew lush and thick branches and needles on one of their sides, yet they were thin, with less branches and needles on the other. He explained that lack of sunshine on the northern side caused less branches and needles to grow on the side with less sun. I felt this was a sorry situation for the poor trees blessed with such a hindrance to their growth. How did they stand a chance to compete for the position of the finest tree in the forest with such a handicap?

I studied on this problem for a while. I had a habit of wandering off to the forest on the side of the mountain above our home whenever I found it uncomfortable to be around my siblings or parents. I could then entertain my own private world where the forest became an enchanted kingdom, and I was a prized visitor from afar. Whereas, the branches, impeding the little paths I would find winding through the forest, littered with little rabbit leavings and deer footprints, would magically swing aside as the trees and bushes ruling the kingdom welcomed me with open arms.

I would talk to the trees, and they would answer back with their whispered swishes and sways and creeks and moans. They told me of turf wars between old craggy stumps and giant powerful trees, and the plights of the many children trees of the kingdom, being born into a world of shade, lack of proper soil for good water retention, and the giant curse of all, being born on a slope where half of them could not grow properly because of lack of sunlight!

Finally, with a proper plan, shovel and water in hand, I set out to remedy this problem once and for all. It would have been an impossible task to move the whole forest. I set out to determine which two young trees most deserved the chance to grow into a future prince or princess of the forest. I carefully interviewed a group of young, excited teen seedlings. I knew they were excited, because, being windy on that day, they seemed to be flapping and flopping and bowing about in a most excitable manner, for trees, that is.

I finally picked two trees. I named one Prince Junior, a most hopeful name, since only the grand old trees can properly pick a true future prince and princess. I named the other tree princess "Juniorette". I set about digging them up. The process was long, fraught with massive roots for such small trees, and many rocks. I finally got the first tree (Prince Junior) dug up. I turned him around so the full branches and leaves faced the north and the sparse branches faced the south. I tucked him gently back into the soil. I watered him generously, and planted a kiss on his one large branch. I completed the second tree removal and turning in about half the time, tapping in the dirt and watering just as my mother was calling for me. I saluted both and promised to water daily for the rest of the summer as I ran down the mountainside. You have to remember. I was just nine years old and, yes, I guess I might have been a bit of a dreamer.

The lucky thing is that someone or something must have been watching over those two poor little trees, because as I visited them daily with a pail of water, I swear they began to thrive. By all accounts, they should have died! It certainly was not the digging up that helped them, but, maybe the watering did. Both trees lived on to be very old trees. As far as I know, they stand together, still.

Chapter 4 - A Lead Creek Turtle

The next summer, I found a turtle crawling on the bank of the river that ran by our home. Now, this was not a normal situation. Turtles do like water, but this river was in no way normal habitat for a turtle. While I was growing up, nothing live could have survived in this river for long. The river was clouded grey with mine tailings, sewage, all manner of garbage from homes, clinkers from several towns' coal furnaces, and dead animals. The only thing that kept life along the river healthy, to a point, were the chemicals that were dumped into the river after being used in the mills to leach minerals from the rocks. Those chemicals were in a kind of strange manner, a counter-balance, which kept some order to an unhealthy system.

I picked up the turtle, (about ten inches long). I turned it over. It had a beautiful painted underside with orange and two toners of green. I noticed a hole in the back of its shell where it had evidently sported a leash at one time. On top of its back, painted in black, was the turtle's name, Mr. Reel. I suppose some fisherman had "reeled" it in while fishing one of the local lakes, and brought it home as a pet. Mr. Reel must not have appreciated being made a pet and devised his escape, only to be apprehended by me!

I made a home for Mr. Reel in the backyard by a small pond. The pond was behind my father's old garage. The garage was made of pine planks and we children used them to write on with chalk, like an outdoors blackboard. I decided to teach Mr. Reel to read.

Now, you have to remember, I was only about ten years old, and had an active imagination. I also knew by that time, that textbooks said animals weren't as intelligent as humans, but I was determined to test the theory.

I spent many hours that summer writing the alphabet and simple words and sounding them out to Mr. Reel. I knew I was making progress, because I noticed he blinked a lot. I told him to blink twice, if he understood, and once if he did not understand. Thereby, we had lots of interesting explanations of words and sounds. He had many things he did not understand, but as I continued throughout each day he either tired, and therefore, blinked more, or he was truly getting it!

One day I came out to feed Mr. Reel and made a huge discovery. Mr. Reel was actually Mrs. Reel. There, by the pond, lay a turtle egg!! Mrs. Reel seemed to know that nothing was to become of the egg, though. She made no attempt to cover it, or care about it. I was about to launch into another ordeal of caring for an egg, when my mother gently explained that there could be no family for Mrs. Reel unless we found Mr. Reel. Mrs. Reel found a solution for herself a couple of weeks later. I went to the pond to find Mrs. Reel to continue her lessons one afternoon. The leash was there. Mrs. Reel was not. Evidently she had tired of her daily school lessons.

Chapter 5 - Junking

I'm thankful that my father liked to work on old cars. In the "old days" before cars had computers, it was a relatively straightforward thing to follow the workings of an engine, transmission, brakes and steering mechanism of a car. If you were reasonably mechanically inclined and put a little time and effort in, you could fix your own car.

Junking, (collecting and selling of old metal), became popular during the second World War when there was a shortage of metals due to production of wartime equipment, tanks, guns, bullets, and so forth.

My father worked in a local mill where precious metals, including; lead, silver, gold, antimony, zinc, tungsten, and copper, bismuth, selenium and tellurium were removed from the ore taken out of the mines. Over 1.2 billion ounces of silver were mined out of Shoshone County, (the heart of the Silver Valley) between 1884 and 2006.

I guess it was natural that, in order to generate extra income for a growing family, my father chose to gather, separate and haul salvage metals to a recycling yard in the big city of Spokane, Washington, about eighty miles away.

One of two main methods he used to gather the metals was to tear apart, down to basic skeletons, old non-working automobiles. He was skilled with a cutting torch, which aided in this task immensely, but caused many a burn on his face, hands and arms. Our mother was constantly forbidding us to go within several feet of this procedure. It was a constant worry for her, and with no wonder, because it was as fascinating as it was dangerous! I still remember the colors of the oxygen and acetylene torch as it hit different metals during the cutting procedure. It appeared as a fireworks display as the sparks flew into the night air when his day was long.

From the time my brother was about nine years old, he assisted my father with tearing apart these old cars. He was usually put to work taking off the simpler parts with a crescent wrench and socket set. By the time he was about twelve years, he was quite a master at taking apart most of the lighter parts of the engines. I followed my brother around like a lost pup any time that I was free from chores. My brother enjoyed the adoration and loved to pass on his knowledge and exercise his importance. He set to teaching me the parts of an engine and made me his "chief assistant". I was quite impressed with the title, and didn't mind handing him the different tools for taking apart the engines, but hated his endless drilling of the parts of the engine. I don't think I was cut out of mechanical cloth, but, in the interest of keeping the title of 'chief assistant', I grudgingly learned all about the sparkplugs, pistons, engine head, head gaskets, fuel pump, piston rings, etc., etc. Each engine came apart. Each car was stripped down. In the process, I found out that I learned a surprising amount about how cars are manufactured, and what makes a car run. I, however, remained a less than enthusiastic student, only appreciating what I had learned later in life, when I found I had developed a taste for classic cars.

Once an old car was torn apart, the real work began. That was the job of sorting the "junk" into piles of salvageable metal by the type. Each type of metal was worth varying amounts. Salvage companies liked the metal clean of other metals, and separated out in individual boxes or piles.

I had a whole new list to learn, but this list I found interesting for some unknown reason. I do and have always been intrigued by different minerals and rocks. The same goes for divining what different metals are composed of. I was so interested and helpful in this process that my father allowed my brother to incorporate my help and I was allowed to have my very own little "junk" pile for pocket money if I helped appreciably with the large family junk pile.

We reclaimed such metal as: pot metal, brass, chrome (not worth much), nickel, lead, copper, iron and aluminum.

One day my brother woke me early in the morning. He had obtained permission from our mother to take me with him. He had found out that the local telephone lines were getting replaced. They were cutting down and rolling up most of the old line, but left pieces large and small all along their path. We started out by our home and worked our way about two miles both ways picking up wire. We must have spent two and a half days on this project, but at the end of each day, tired and hungry, and very dirty, we had a large pile of copper wire.

The next thing we had to do was to separate the copper wire from the coating on the outside. This was accomplished by making a great bonfire and placing the wire in the fire. After the fire burned down, only the copper was left. You had to be careful not to let the fire burn too hot, though, or you would melt the copper! The fire was always fun, but we got plenty black and had to have baths right away when we came into the house.

Another way we got junk was a little on the sneaky side. Our parents forbid us to go down by the river. It ran fast in the spring, and, even though in the middle of the summer, it ran low and would have been hard to drown in, it was very unhealthy because of all the sewage, garbage and mine waste that went into it. Because of all the garbage that went into it, however, it made a wonderful treasure trove of junk metal. My brother got in the habit of sneaking off with me in tow to collect junk. We did pretty well, especially in the aluminum collection, and aluminum had a pretty good price on it. When the junk was collected to a sufficient amount, Dad would haul the scrap into Spokane in a pickup or the "big" truck. At times, he used these trips for a chance to "get away" with our mother for a few hours and to have dinner at a roadside diner on the way home. Many times, though, our mother could not get away because of needs of one or more of us children. At these times, Dad took turns taking one or more of us children with him. Our older brother got preference since he was his chief helper. I had second preference of sorts, since I had some of the junk involved and was my brother's "chief assistant". I loved these trips. The sights and sounds of the "big" city of Spokane fascinated me. Watching the large magnet on a crane picking up the scrap iron out of my father's pickup was always thrilling. I always held my breath just before the magnet picked up the scrap out of the pickup. It was a secret fear of mine that It would miss and pick up the whole pickup with me in it!

Getting to stop at a roadside café and order a hamburger and milkshake after the truck was unloaded was the highlight of the trip. I really don't care for hamburgers that much, but I can still taste the flavor of those hamburgers, French fries and chocolate shakes! This went well for a couple of summers and I will always treasure that bit of time I had with my brother and father in the "junking" trade. However, the price of junk metal is volatile, children grow, my father's odd jobs became more consuming and for many years he did more tearing down of old mills and buildings and saved the hauling of junk metals for a future time. My brother got old enough to take on odd jobs of his own. It also was no longer "cool" to be tagged around by a bothersome little sister and I became a young teenager with more household duties, and a summer babysitting job of my own.

Chapter 6 - A Pool of Thought

Our home was built by an old miner soon after the 1910 fire. It was built right off the side of the original old highway that actually ran just behind our house. We used to play on what was termed "the old road bed", which was gradually reclaimed by the ever moving mountain behind us. Our house, we found in later years was built beside a garbage dump of sorts, since, while excavating at the side of the house, we found a huge treasure trove of old jars, bottles, pieces of old furniture and what-not. The old bottles were quite entertaining, having names of special elixirs claiming to work untold wonders on the human body. Amazing what a traveling salesman had inside his black bag in those days!

The front yard of our home was a pile, or many piles of dredged rocks, where owners before our time had dredged out and "re-run" tailings, (digging out and shipping to smelters the mine waste that had washed down-river and collected in the rocks). In the old days, (before 1969 and the National Environmental Policy Act), the amount of mine waste, and missed minerals that washed into the river was probably substantial. I remember playing on these piles of rocks with my older brother and sister. Over the years, my father brought in fresh dirt from my grandparent's ranch on the North Fork of the Coeur d'Alene. He also moved dirt from our mountain with his tractor and brought the level of the land up and created a fresh bed for plants and trees to grow in, turning the barren landscape of the 1940s into a lush garden by the 1960s. One hole, however, was deeper and slower to be filled in. I don't think it was a planned thing. I just think our father had left that part to deal with to last as he had no immediate need for the land. He had fashioned a built-up driveway around the area, and in the interim, he used the "hole" to store extra scrap iron. My mother was always "after him" to do something about the "hole" because she was afraid one of the "little kids" would venture out and fall on the rocks or scrap iron piled up. One day, after studying the situation, my father came up with his solution. The price of concrete was at an all-time low. He had just torn down an old water "flume" (aqueduct for carrying water), made of excellent two by ten lumber. The clincher for the decision was that it had been an extraordinarily high water year and my mother was once again expounding on the dangers of the nearby river and the fact that the only swimmer in the family was my father. Our father decided that the hole was an excellent spot for a swimming pool! He set about cutting up and hauling off all the old scrap iron to the Spokane junk yards.

As the leaves came out on the trees and the butterflies spread their fresh yellow and black wings out of their cocoons, my father was found in the hole, with my brother as his helper, as he formed up a square swimming pool thirty feet long, twenty four feet wide and four feet tall. He put in a pipe for a drain hole at the south end and slanted the floor slightly for drainage on that end. He left an open rock hole still on the south side of the pool for water to collect when it drained, where it would gradually seep into the rocks, under the dike road and into the river. It was quite a project. The large concrete trucks came in and dumped loads of concrete. He lined us older children along the wall. We were given long thin sticks. My father and mother also had long sticks. We all pounded the cement and gravel mix down into the forms after the trucks were dumped so there would be not as many air "pockets" in the concrete. Our pool turned out a sensational success! Our father pushed dirt up and around the sides. He gradually spray-painted the inside a blue green color and we girls painted under sea designs on the sides of the pool. He later put a slab of cement on the north side of the pool that was great to lie on in the mid-day sun. He also dumped sand on the other side of the concrete slab so the "little kids" could play in the sand. The water for the pool came straight off the mountain. It came from a clear, cold, mineral sweet stream, fresh from under the ground. You can imagine the shock jumping in the middle of March in the mountains! It became a family tradition.

A few weeks after the pool was finished, our father came home to announce that he was told by someone in the assessor's office that we had the honor of having the first "private" swimming pool in the county!

Father was not done with construction on the pool, however. He got thinking that the pool would be even better if we only had a little heat. He had an old tractor steam engine boiler sitting in his iron pile waiting to be cut up. He got his tractor out and pulled the old boiler down the road till it set at the south end of the pool just on the other side of the hole left for pool drainage. He then attached an old water tank to the boiler and ran the water through the tank. He stoked up the steam boiler and heated up the water tank and ran the steam water into the pool. It worked like a charm, but worried our parents on many fronts. First, the water that came out was hotter than hot! It would scorch the skin off a buffalo in a minute flat! The second problem was that there was no pressure gauge on the steam boiler or the water tank any more. That steam boiler got mighty hot when it was stoked up. Our father was a little leery that he could blow the steam boiler, the tank or everything. It was just too dangerous and he stopped warming up the pool almost as soon as he started. I only remember one or two trial runs.

The next summer, my father came up with the final plan. It was really wonderful and took no extra labor or worry, except the water could still get mighty hot! He had torn down an old building with a very large pipe radiator of sorts. The complete structure made of parallel pipes zigzagging back and forth about two and a half feet tall and twenty-four feet long. He stood it on the north side of the pool for the best southern exposure. He hooked the hose that brought the water to fill the pool from the mountain to the one end of the pipe. He attached another hose with a faucet on the other end. The water would sit in the pipe until it warmed. We could then open up the faucet and let extremely warm water into the pool. Between the sun-warmed water and the natural warming effect of the sun on the pool in the summer, we had fairly warm water throughout the summer. The pool drain was small and it took time to drain, and clean. We usually had to clean the pool about once a month because of the leaves, dust, and dirt that would blow in the pool. There was no filtration system like pools now have to filter things out. It usually took about two days to fully drain the pool. We kids would then climb into the pool and wash and sweep the walls with bleach and water mix. The bottom of the pool was swept and any dirt or debris was picked up with a dustpan, not swept down the drain. The pool was then rinsed thoroughly and re-filled. It was a dangerous "pit" for the "little kids" while it was slowly filling. We had to watch that the "little kids" didn't wander too close and fall four feet to the hard concrete bottom while it was being cleaned. One time we came out in the morning to find a deer running around in about foot and a half of water. Dad got an old plank and put in the pool for her to jump up on and get out, which she did in short order, bouncing off to the forest like she had springs.

That swimming pool taught us some interesting social lessons. If you have something that no one else around you has, do not display it in plain sight, or be willing to share it with your friends. The pool sat in plain view, across the river from the highway that went into town. My parents were basically shy and very private. I guess they were pretty overwhelmed and worn out most of the time by raising seven children, even though, I don't doubt they enjoyed us and certainly provided interesting entertainment and educational opportunities for us. The rule, basically, was, as I have said before, that we had each other for friends while we were at home, and our parents did not see the need to "import" friends for us to play with. This meant that there would be no inviting of friends to swim. Well, rules were made to be broken, and it took no time at all for reactions to this rule. The best case scenario came from close neighbor children just "showing up" with swimming suits on once in a while. This was always great fun, because, once there, our father ignored them, and our mother would allow them to stay and play with us in the pool and even feed them! Wow! It was great to have friends over!

The negative side of this rule was that resentments built up. I can remember one late evening when we heard loud car noises outside in the dark. Our father was home and went out, we children following behind. There was a car loaded with about three of my older sister's classmates that lived just around the mountain going crazily around and around the pool. They were shouting mean things and throwing beer cans in the pool. Father shouted back at them and they drove off, car weaving crazily on the way. We were worried they would drive off our old crooked bridge. They didn't, but our father was angry for quite a time. We older children were just embarrassed.

33

If parents have rules about not inviting friends, it can affect friendships in other ways, too. Sisters and brothers are best of friends. It is a love and a friendship that lasts forever. You cannot "divorce" or not be friends of some sort with a sister or brother even if you are a lot different, or even if you do not agree with them. It just is. There is some intangible tie that binds you forever. A love for a best friend can be very similar, but is tied by common likes and feelings, and reciprocation, and the sharing of experiences, good and bad. I had and still have "best friends" from childhood, but I understood from about junior high age that my "best" friends were somewhat one-sided. They could be my "best" friends, but on the other side, my "best" friend would probably find another "best" friend that would in turn have her over to visit at her house, invite her to parties and do sleepovers with her, all of which was not allowed for me. I will say that parenting is a continual learning process, and with my younger siblings, rules changed on some issues.

The summer after the eighth grade, I had two "best friends". I hung out with the both of them at our school. One of my best friends invited me to a spectacular Halloween party which I was allowed to attend. By the time school was ready to get out for the summer, I felt it was about time I "reciprocated". The problem was, it was not really "allowed" to have friends over. Well, things took care of themselves. One beautiful early summer day, my two friends came walking down our road, suntanned in shorts, swimsuits and towels in hand. They had decided a visit was in order and had told their parents they were invited for a swim. Honestly, the "particulars" escape me, the eventual repercussions do not. A conversation before school let out, I believe went a little like the following; "So, what would your mom do if we just showed up?"

"Well, probably nothing, and it would be really fun!"

34

"Well, okay, so YOU wouldn't mind if we just showed up?"

"Oh, heck, no!"

"Well, maybe, then, we just might show up!"

So, when they did "just show up", we had a deliriously super great time! I felt like the luckiest girl alive! My siblings enjoyed the company too! They stayed for several hours. I had hopes that this was just the first of many such visits. I was wondering why I hadn't thought of them "just showing up" before! Life was beautiful! Well, that is, until they crossed the crooked bridge on their way back home.

I was in trouble! My mother's face changed from one of a sweet understanding, welcoming mother to that of an accusing, not so happy, parent! I tried to explain that that I had not actually straight out "invited" them. I explained that they had just decided to show up like the neighbor kids did sometimes. It didn't work. The belt appeared, and needless to say, my bottom was sore for a bit. I never regretted that visit from my friends. It remained a treasured memory.

We all learned to swim and spent many hot summer days playing in that pool. The first swim in the spring was still a shock!

Chapter 7 - Tie Rods Are Not For Fishing

About 1959, when the whole family would go out to the ranch on the north fork of the Coeur d'Alene River, where my Grandmother and Grandfather lived, we would ride in the pickup. Now, there were nine of us, total, at that time. My youngest sister had just turned one year old that spring, and I would turn eleven in the fall. No way would all of us fit in the front cab of that old pickup! All of us older children, this time, including the fourth child in line, Dana, (four years younger than I), got to sit in the bed of the pickup. This was really great fun on warm summer days. You could feel the cool breeze from the shaded gullies washing up and over the road as we passed by. You could smell the scents of ripening huckleberries, old cedars, and rich honeysuckles loaded with dewy honey. You would also get covered in dust as cars passed by, but that was just all part of the fun and excitement. I felt sorry for the passengers up front, including my father, (the driver), my mother, my little brother, Danny, little sister, Kate, and baby sister, Natalie, for having to be stuck in the stuffy old cab.

In those days, they didn't have pickups with a second seat behind the driver's. There was just one, long, front seat. The back window didn't even open. That wasn't an option yet, either. Most pickups had rifle racks for their hunting rifles over the back window. It was more normal than not to see pickups parked in downtown Wallace with hunting rifles with nice scopes sitting in racks up against the back window of the truck cab. These rifles were toted all year around, even to high school, in case the owner wished to go hunting after school got out.

The pickup was about a 1954 vintage. Once you started over Dobson pass to go from the South Fork of the Coeur d'Alene River, the road turned into a gravel road with more than a few pot holes from wear. It was a curvy road, so I was glad we were riding in the back, because I didn't seem to get car sick if I had enough fresh air to breathe.

We usually stopped about half way down the hill to give everyone a break, and check out the ripeness of the berries which would be ready to pick each year about the end of July. There was also a fountain with fresh mountain stream water running at the side of the road. The forest service had built up a little rock encasement and turned it into a drinking fountain that ran continuously. Drivers also used this to add water to their radiators if their car heated up coming over the mountain.

The Forest Service employee that built that fountain was a true artist when it came to building rock structures. He did a beautiful job with this fountain. He also built a rock wall on a U.S. Forest Service constructed hiker's trail that goes to Revett Lake, a beautiful little lake on the Montana, Idaho border off the Thompson Pass highway that goes from the North Fork of the Coeur 'd Alene to Thompson Falls, Montana. I would recommend this hike to anyone who loves hiking and discovering pristine mountain lakes. It is only about a 2 mile hike into the lake, and easy hiking. The rock wall runs along a portion of the trail and has held up well over the years. It was originally built about 1968.

Back then, the Forest Service hired crews in the summer to clean and burn brush, and create hiking trails, clear forest service roads and stand available for fire suppression. They worked out of Forest Service Camps. If they were working very far out, they might just camp in forest service tents on site.

The men that camped were usually young college students. They didn't have cell phones or computers or 'IPads' or 'IPods' to entertain them in the evenings, so they had to rely on invention. The local wood rats seemed to think these camps were made just for them and regularly invaded the tents at night.

Old wood dynamite boxes were easy to come by since dynamite was not highly regulated in those days and it was used quite commonly not only in the building of roads, but in mining. Some of the workers dreamed up a quite effective "rat flattener", (as it was referred to). They took an old dynamite box and loaded it with rocks. They propped it up inside their tent between their beds. They tied a string to the stick the box was propped up with and put crumbs under the box. They would then lie in their beds waiting for an unsuspecting wood rat to come along looking for a meal and pull the string which released the stick and flattened the rat. It was a very effective means of rodent control. I never was able to confirm if it was condoned by the Forest Service.

After our family left the water fountain on Dobson Pass, we were looking forward to a nice swim on the North Fork River at our grandparent's place. Dad headed out in the pickup at a pretty good clip and hit the first curve. The pickup made a clunking sound and slid on the gravel, careening to the outside of the road, (which gave us kids in the back, a jolt and an extremely nice view of the drop off on that side and the valley below). Just then, there was another louder clunk and a thump and we scrunched to a stop. We came to rest with one tire at the very edge of the road, but safe for the time being, as it rested against a stump. Mom and the little kids had to get out on Dad's side. He warned all of us kids in back to climb out carefully up by the cab on the left. Dad inspected the pickup and announced that we had broken a tie rod. I thought rods were for fishing, and tying was for flies!

We all got a lesson in tie rods on cars and how important they are for steering. Dad explained that when we skidded, he found that when the tie rod went on the front left wheel, it broke the brake line. He had no front tire and no brakes for a moment. He quickly pulled the emergency brake, which caused the rear tires to lock and pull us to a stop.

Wow! He also explained that if we hadn't stopped at the water fountain, we probably would have been going too fast for everything to work right. We all went to the side of the road and looked over and the drop off. That would have been quite a ride, or roll. I'm glad we stopped for water!

There were no cell phones in those days, and there was not much traffic on the road. We were left to our own devices. Father proceeded to cut a piece of baling wire he had in the back of the pickup. He used the wire to tie the tie rod back in place. An old gentleman happened by and pulled us back onto the road. We still had no brakes. The transmission in the pickup was manual. Father shifted down to the lowest gear and crawled down the mountain with us, gently using the emergency brake when he had to. It was a long trip, but we made it to our grandparents in one piece!

North Fork of the Coeur d'Alene, Shoshone Work Camp USFS, 1970s

North Fork of the Coeur d'Alene River

Chapter 8 – Planting Buildings

Most people that have land, plant crops. My father planted buildings. The summer of 1959, I had just finished the sixth grade. My father contracted to tear down or move some old Northern Pacific railway buildings. I was too young to remember many of the details, except the ones that affected our family in a big way. The first thing I remember was the announcement that we were going to have a cabin on the land that my parents had purchased from our grandparents in Sandpoint. The land laid on the edge of an estuary to Lake Pend Oreille.

The "cabin" was to be a red boxcar that needed to be removed from the railroad yards in Wallace. Our father set to work with my brother, Jimmy. He jacked up the boxcar that was already off the tracks and on a foundation of sorts. After the boxcar was jacked up and blocked on large timbers, he hired a friend that owned a small flat-bed eighteen-wheeler to haul it. His friend was a talented driver and backed right under the boxcar on the first try! After that, it was a simple job of dropping the boxcar down on the flatbed and securing it with chains. My brother was lucky enough to ride shotgun with the semi-driver. I was too young to be allowed to go. My father drove a pickup with a wide-load sign ahead of the boxcar all the way to Sandpoint which was usually about a two and a half hour trip, about 100 miles. The trip with the boxcar took about six hours. My cousin and his wife drove a pickup behind the semi truck with another wide load sign. The scariest part of the trip was that they had to watch for overhead wires in towns. In those days, there was no interstate, more towns to go through and a few railroad overpasses that they barely fit under!

That boxcar turned out to be the greatest cabin! We had a kitchen, dining area, a bathroom and a large sleeping area with beds set up along the walls. We were able to visit our grandparents and family in Sandpoint more often with the cabin. As we got older, we older children were allowed to stay at the cabin for about three days alone each summer, as long as we reported several times a day to our grandparents or aunt and uncle, who all lived nearby. The land the cabin was on laid on the edge of an estuary to Lake Pend Oreille, dubbed "Chuck's Slough". We would catch frogs and perch. We would turn the frogs loose and cook the perch. I can still remember the sun sifting through the worn boxcar window in the morning with the red checkered curtains my mother had sewn. At night, I would lie in the squeaky metal bed and listen to the sound of the Great Northern train, its long eerie whistle as it streamed across the long bridge that crossed Lake Pend Oreille on the other side of town. I can still feel the morning fog wrapping itself like a weightless veil across my shoulders, branches brushing my hair as I pick my way along the muddy bank of the slough, willow pole in hand, cotton string dangling from the end of the pole, safety pin on the end, slimy angle worms in my pocket, hands still smelling of wet clay earth from angle worm "mining". When I was in Sandpoint, I never wanted to go back home. As soon as we went home, I was glad I was back. The familiar welcomed me.

Our landscape changed at home, that summer, too. Our father hauled a small shop from the railroad yards to settle on the "old road bed" to the east of our house. The shop was about twenty-four feet by twelve feet and he hauled it in on one of his flatbed trucks without much trouble.

The next building he hauled in from the railroad yards was larger. It was about twenty feet by twenty eight feet. The

42

haul of that building was much more interesting. It took two flatbed trucks and two drivers. My brother, (just 15 years old), drove the front truck, my father drove the back truck. The back truck backed while the front truck went frontwards. They inched their way along a back road and across our bridge. Mother thought the bridge was going to go down under the weight of the two trucks and the house. My dad had explained that the weight would be distributed so that not too much weight would be in one place at once. I guess he was right. The house made it to its resting spot. We had one more building on our place.

The ice house was the last building our father moved from the railroad yards instead of tearing it down. He was running out of time. The weather was getting colder and the snow would soon be upon us. We were also running out of room to put buildings! The ice house was really tall, standing about twenty feet tall at the peak of the roof. It was very heavy because it had an attic filled with about two and a half feet of sawdust with sawdust in the walls about a foot thick for insulation. It measured about twenty-two feet by twenty four feet.

My mother knew that this building would truly be the demise of our father, our bridge, and possibly her oldest son. Our father persisted, amidst protests from our mother. We all watched as, once again, Father's two flat-bed trucks, one going forward, one going backward, inched their way along a back road towards our little bridge. I swear, as he traversed the little bridge, I saw it shudder as the first truck hit the mid-section. He never got it further than a flat field area just west of the bridge. There was no room on our land to take it further, and a grove of trees just to the west of it. It sat there propped up on timbers, old gray, tarpapered sides, for many years.

I got quite fond of that large ice house. I was just beginning my teenage years. Sometimes I just needed a place to be alone. That ice house attic, being lined with sawdust, was quiet, cool, and soft. The best place to hide from the world. It was cool in the summer, and always kept above freezing in the attic in the winter.

When I-90 came through in the late 1970's, it took our little bridge, made crooked by floods and years of carrying huge weights, and a large chunk of our land. Our father was then able to move the ice house to its final resting spot as his garage, and give it a facelift.

The one building our father tore totally down in the railroad yards was a brick roundhouse. It was torn down earlier than the other buildings, in about 1959. It was not a large roundhouse. It was built with six bays, or garages for six railroad steam engines. It had a turntable in front of it. The walls of the roundhouse were about eighteen inches thick of brick and mortar. My brother was mostly my father's only helper. The rest of us children weren't allowed near when he was taking the walls down because it was too dangerous. They hitched a long cable around the wall and hooked it to my father's little yellow Caterpillar twenty-eight. My brother later explained to me that it took many attempts to begin rocking the wall. He said that once it started rocking, my father just kept backing and tugging a little more each time until the whole wall caved. He said that when it did cave, he had to scramble for his life, and my father only missed getting his tractor and himself covered by bricks by inches. It was just lucky that the cable was a long one! After the first wall caved, the others came down easier. After the bricks were down, all of we older children, even our mother, helped load bricks in pickups and trucks to haul. Once we had them home and stacked, father used some of them to make us a large patio that still stands today.

We sold many of the bricks. Father charged three cents a brick for cleaned, and two and a half cents a brick for un-cleaned (with the mortar still on). We children cleaned a lot of them, with a hammer and chisel. Father paid us a half cent a brick to clean.

Many years later, my husband and I hauled some of the old roundhouse bricks to southern Idaho. We built a brick house with bricks spotted in throughout the structure from the roundhouse.

The roundhouse was originally built in Wallace after the 1910 fire. It is hard to find a picture of the old roundhouse, which was six bays, for six old steam engines, with a round table in front. Usually, the old pictures of Wallace were taken from the east looking west, and from a location that just misses the roundhouse area, because of the mountains. I do, however, have some old postcards, one from the 1930s, and another about 1959, just before the roundhouse was torn down, that do show it in the distance.

Chapter 9 - A Record of Sorts or a Sort of Records

Imagine being able to play any one of ten-thousand 78 rpm records from the 1930s, 1940s and early 1950. That is a lot of records. That is the number of records estimated that my father hauled home from his next job, a year later. The railroad house (office) seemed the perfect place to put the records in their shelves. Actually, there weren't 10,000 different phonograph records; there were many copies of one record, from one to about five to seven.

The building was owned by A.F. Mc Fee. He had a business called the North Idaho Sales Company. It supplied slot machines, juke boxes and the records for the juke boxes. My father had salvage rights which included the ten thousand records. We ended with one one-armed bandit, and an old juke box that didn't work. We used the one-armed bandit as a bank. Whenever Dad had quarters, he would give them for us kids to plug in and pull the arm. When he was short money, he would dump the one arm bandit.

We children became well versed in all the old 78 songs and record labels. There were a lot of pre-war and war songs, Bing Crosby tunes, and Rosemary Clooney songs like "Come On-A My House". The Texas Rangers had war tunes like "I Changed My Penthouse for a Pup Tent", Guy Lombardo and his Orchestra had vintage songs like "An Old Country Garden". Oh, yes, I can't forget my favorite records out of the collection. Those would be the ones Doris Day sang. Labels included Paramount records, Capitol, RCA, DECCA, Victor, Columbia, Diamond, Linden, London, Tops, Okeh and Atlantic. The records' looks were varied. Some were shiny black, (the newer vinyl ones from the 50s). Some were a dull black, and there were some red vinyl. The dull black records were made of shellac and ground slate and broke and chipped quite easily. We had an old phonograph in the "record house" as it was dubbed. We would go out and play old records for hours. Father put us to work inventorying the records, but the job was never finished. We grew up too fast!

Some Records from the North Idaho Sales Company Building

Chapter 10 - Toyderytown, Alaska

My sisters, brothers and I lived an idyllic life of pretend in that we were fortunate enough to have the resources to put our childhood fantasies to life.

We had the river, where many forms of garbage were flung. We had the land with its hidden away places nestled against the mountain, secreted away from prying eyes and the necessity of entertaining ourselves with no neighborhood friends or television for distraction. We also had a large supply of random articles from our father's endless jobs, tearing apart old cars, tearing down old buildings, doing handyman work for local homeowners, and collecting usable items from the town dump. He also was continually remodeling and adding on to our home, which was small for a family of seven children. Our father bought things he needed in a large supply at times, like the pile of sand that ended up in our side yard. You have to remember, though, our side yard was about seven acres large. The sand pile was supposed to be used exclusively for his concrete making jobs. Over time, however, it became a play place for our play construction equipment, sand buckets shovels, and other treasures.

One summer, when my brother was about twelve years old, and I about nine, we decided to build a "real" construction company, with garages for our construction vehicles. We constructed it of old bricks for the sides and pieces of old plywood for the roofs. After playing for several weeks, digging with our trucks, moving dirt, rocks and sand, my brother came up with a game changing idea. He had been helping our father mix concrete. He noticed that, careful as father was, some of the raw cement was always left on the ground by the mixer and around the bags. We started scooping up this raw cement, which we mixed with sand and water and poured into miniature forms which outlined sidewalks for our future town! When the sidewalks dried, they outlined the skeleton framework for a small miniature town behind our father's garage. The total size of the town would be about ten feet long, streets about fourteen inches wide, with sidewalks two inches on either side. Our wooden stores would fill in on either side of the street, making the entire width about forty inches wide. Outside the town was a miniature pond, we designated a lake. Just above, on the hillside, was a mound of dirt with a little path (we called it a "dirt road"). This was about a foot wide. There was a nice flat place under the shade of a large elderberry bush on top of the mound, tucked in against the mountain. That became the perfect place for my "farm". That winter my brother started learning to use our father's table saw. By spring, he was able to use our father's table saw on his own. Our "town" was turning into more of a small scale hobby. He decided to see if he could construct some real small scale houses and stores. The first attempt was a twenty-six inch tall and twenty inch wide, three-story hotel we named the "Ritz". I painted it with some old blue paint and lettered the words "Ritz" (borrowed from a cracker box). The next was a grocery store carved out of a wooden apple box with roof added and door and windows carved out with a saber saw. It became the local market. The filling station was next, made with the help of two by four boards, a hand saw, some nails and old boards for a roof. It was time to name our town. By that time, we had enlisted our younger sisters and brother, put up telephone poles along the sidewalk, strung old copper wire for lights, run by an old car battery, and hired a town "physician" named Sam Johnson (my alias). We decided we not only had to have a town name, we also had to know what state it was in. We decided that since in the winter, there would be mounds of snow by the small town's standards, it should be a state with gallons of snow! Therefore, the state became the state of Alaska. The town's name came from what we were doing, playing with toys!

Our town was christened, Toyderytown, Alaska. The local grocery was Toyderytown Market.

It was Sam Johnson's job to make "people" out of old pipe cleaners. I fashioned "babies", "men", "women", and "teenagers" with different sizes of pipe cleaners. Every child who participated could make up their own family and vocation. After that, if any people were to be added, they had to make up a story-line of where they came from, their vocation, and where they would live. If a family were to be expanded, they had to talk it over with the town doctor who then would announce the date of the birth and present the proud parents with their child or children. Children could "grow". It is easy to scrunch or stretch pipe cleaner "children". Cloths were fashioned out of small scraps of cloth, and a clothing store was added. Groceries in the grocery store consisted of elderberries which were melons, miniature cut-outs of colored cardboard for cans and boxes, tiny scraps of leaves for lettuce and greenery. Hay for the farm was dried lawn grass which was stored on the "farm" in miniature "haystacks". We regularly combed the banks of the river where we would occasionally find a discarded plastic farm animal or military horse. One time we really made a find with a sheep, a man and a baby. That grey river was full of treasures! We also obtained several old cars, a boat and some plastic doll furniture that fit into our town.

On my birthday, that September, my brother surprised me with one of my most memorable birthday gifts. A handmade farmhouse dollhouse for my farm! He had put it together much like a real home is built, with hand cut miniature planks. It even had a deck off the top floor. The roof was shingled in miniature shake roofing. I loved that doll house and my farm. All of us learned a bucketful of life from that miniature town. I still have a picture of that miniature town stored in my mind; all lit up at Christmastime, with streets "plowed". We spent untold hours playing "real life" and have referred to our experiences in that play "town life" often in our adult life as it felt as if we had already lived a practice version of some of the real experiences in life in that real toy town.

Chapter 11 - The River Rats

One of the more exciting and forbidden things we did as children, together, was a game we named "River Ratting". We dubbed ourselves secretly, "The River Rats".

The game started one day while our parents were away. It was the middle of summer and too warm to be indoors. Our older sister, Lana, discovered Jimmy, Dana, I, walking along the river, looking for discarded toys, such as toy cars or trucks, doll furniture, or toy soldiers Toyderytown, or scrap metal such as aluminum pie plates, pieces of scrap iron, or pieces of copper wire. Garage sales were a rarity back in the early 1960s. Most people just threw unwanted items in the trash. The trash, more often than not, was the river. Many times we would find balls of different sizes washed up along the banks to add to our play collection.

Lana or "Sissy", as we called her, was as excited as a bantam hen, running about the riverbank, shouting threats that we were really "in for it" when our parents got home, if we hadn't drowned before. My brother was good at making his case. In no time, "Sissy" was convinced that we three were having the adventure of our lives and that it might just be a good idea if she and the three "little ones" should come join us.

Truthfully, there was little danger of us drowning in the middle of the summer, in that gray river. It was running at a fairly low level, maybe three feet in the middle of the channel where it narrowed. The edges we walked on were dry flats out at least two to four feet in most areas and twelve feet in others, with about six inch deep shores in most. There was more danger falling and hitting a boulder and being washed downstream unconscious.

The fact that the gray waters were not healthy for us did not totally escape us. We, however, decided that thoroughly cleaning with soap and water whatever we "claimed" from the river mud, washed to the shores, would suffice. We also made sure we washed up after our outings. In those days, (the early 1960s), long term health risks possibly derived from the river's contents was not a newsworthy item.

Down the river bank came "Sissy" with the "little kids" in tow. We all took turns carrying the youngest, Natalie, and keeping a hand on, Danny and Kate. What a great adventure it was! We walked along the river on our side to the crooked bridge. Under the bridge, we rested in the cool shade the giant bridge timbers offered, feeling the soft breeze of the creek as the water flowed over the rocks and crashed against the huge pillars made of ancient steam boilers.

We discovered that the old railroad ties that shored up the ends of the bridge made an excellent hiding place for toys found, that needed to be brought home at another convenient time for washing and "blending" into our toy collection. We found a doll that day. The "little kids" were excited and wanted to take it home that day. It was in pretty good condition for the ride down the river it had endured. The doll fed everyone's imagination about "adopting" a "discarded" child.

We ventured on beyond the bridge. Our land consisted of two separate deeds. One deed contained our home and the land to the bridge. The other deed was land to the east of the bridge. We referred to it as the "old place". This second piece of land, about forty acres along the mountainside, had originally been an old homestead. Father had purchased it from the original owner before he purchased our place. The homestead house, (by this time, a shamble of boards, was built over a stream that tumbled down the mountain and into the river. Across from the stream there was a field and an orchard with plums, pears and apples.

The old highway road bed that ran along the north mountain, through where we lived, mostly disguised by trees and bushes, reappeared above the bridge head. We came up from the river bottom on the other side of our bridge, still on the north shore. We continued along and up to the "old place" where we had a wonderful afternoon picking plums (which were the only thing ripe at the time). We drank from the cool mountain stream, and checked out the old tumbled down ruins of the house before we returned home.

When Mother and Father returned, we told them about the trip to the "old place". This was allowed, on occasion, as long as "Sissy", who was "in charge", authorized it. We never included the "river ratting" in the disclosure. River ratting would stay our secret for many years.

The adopted doll did come into question by our parents later, when he turned up in a doll bed. The simple explanation was, that we saw it by the river bank on the way home from school and ran down and rescued him. That sufficed. We received a short scolding on the dangers of such a rescue, and that was that. "You just don't mess with some things that don't need messing with!"

Chapter 12 - North Idaho's First "Moon Launch"

The Soviet made Sputnik 1 was the first Earth satellite made by man. It was a polished metal sphere, twenty-three inches in diameter, with four external radio antennas to broadcast radio pulses. It was launched into orbit around the Earth by the Soviets on October 4, 1957. It could be seen from Earth and had detectable radio pulses. As a result of the success of Sputnik 1, Americans were thrown into a "Sputnik crisis" of sorts. This also began the official race into space between the United States and the Soviet Union, and was an integral a part of the ensuing "Cold War". January 31, 1958, the United States launched our first satellite, Explorer I into orbit around the Earth. It was pencil shaped, eighty inches long and about six and a quarter inches in diameter. In 1959, with the Luna 2, the first non-powered Moon landing was achieved by the Soviets. In 1962, the United States achieved a similar mission to the moon, with an astronaut-less moon landing of the space craft Ranger IV.

By October 1962, As a result of these dynamic advances in space exploration and communications, everyone was caught up in the excitement of the possibility of life in outer space and the launching of spacecraft.

I was an eighth grader in 1962. My brother was in the tenth grade, and our oldest sister was a senior. We all rode the same bus to school and home daily. A bus filled with smells of bologna sandwiches, smashed bananas, hairspray and chili farts, bubble gummed floors, spit-balled windows and screaming kids. We came home from school one rainy day in the middle of October to find a large silver "rocket" sitting upright in a wood crated frame in our front driveway. It was about twelve feet tall with small wings and tail fins at the back. It stood silently gazing at the sky as waiting to be called to the stars beckoning above. We were in awe. Where had this mysterious craft come from, and how could we have been picked to host its extraordinary presence?

Our mother explained to us that our father had brought it home on his truck from a junk yard in Spokane, Washington. He had hauled a load of scrap metal in to the junk yard early that morning. Evidently, for reasons unknown to us, he had taken some of his pay in trade for the "rocket". Our father explained later that the craft was not a "rocket", but an airplane "drop tank". He explained that aircraft like the F-86 Sabre during the Korean War would carry extra fuel in these aluminum "rockets". When they drained the fuel from the tanks, they could jettison them, or "drop" the tanks into the ocean. They were later picked up by ships to be recycled for their aluminum. Some tanks, such as the one my father traded for, were surplus, never used before the F-86 was de-commissioned.

Our father loved to read. He read everything he could get his hands on about satellites and the space race. He was intrigued by the rocket, and had an interesting plan for his new acquisition.

Before leaving for school the next day, our father advised us that if anyone asked about the shiny silver rocket in our driveway, we should tell them that the rocket was scheduled for a launch to the moon on Halloween night.

Amazing! Who would guess high school and junior high students have such keen eyesight! Yep. No sooner had we boarded the bus in the morning than the questions began.

"What's that silver thing in your yard?"

"Do you have a ROCKET in your yard?"

"Does your dad work for NASA?"

"Is it LEGAL to have a rocket?"

"What are you going to DO with the rocket?"

Well, it was something different to talk about, for sure! We fielded all the questions. It actually became fun making up embellishments to the tale. Basically, we told them that our dad had decided to launch the rocket on his own and had put it together in his garage until it was about ready to launch. We told them, as our father had instructed, that it was scheduled to "launch" on Halloween night, and that his goal was to hit the moon. We heard a lot of kids on the bus say that it would NEVER go that far, but all were ready and waiting to watch for the launch on Halloween night. Personally, I had no idea how our father was going to "pull it off"!

By Halloween night, our father had gathered together a massive pile of old boards from an old building he was tearing down. After dark, he poured gas on the massive pile of boards and lit the fire. He threw on some old tires for good measure. Huge plumes of dark smoke went up. Bright orange flames licked up to kiss the low hanging clouds of smoke and sparks flew. I have never seen such a glorious bonfire! In the midst of smoke and flames, our father pulled the standing rocket down and removed it from its crate prison. He burned the crate in the fire. He took the rocket and placed it behind the shed, where it was out of sight.

The next day we were surprised to find that most of the kids on the bus had evidently talked their parents into driving by to see the "launch". All were believers. Most were in awe. We were too. Our father had actually pulled it off! The rocket had evidently missed the moon. No headlines touted our blazing success. It most likely circled the earth, or was shot down by the "Commies", but, no matter...we were launched into the space race. Anything was possible. We looked forward to the conversation on the bus. It smelled a little less of foul odors, our shoes slid deftly over the bubble gum and orange peels, and our eyes looked far beyond the spit balled windows.

In the spring, our father pulled the abandoned rocket out from the snow behind the shed. He got out his cutting torch and cut two holes in the middle of it, one in the front half and one in the back half. The holes were about two feet long and two feet wide. They were just big enough for a child to climb in and pretend like they were going for a ride, like in a play airplane. Our father attached a chain to the front and the back of the "rocket". Father had welded together a "motor puller" for pulling out and repairing car motors a few years before. The motor puller had been standing in the side-yard, a gawky, thirteen foot tall pipe spider, unused since the last motor was repaired. The motor puller was basically old pipe with a crossbar and four spread legs, welded to look like a large swing with no swing hanging down in the middle. Father hoisted the rocket up where a swing would be. We now had a rocket swing. The younger children in the family really enjoyed that rocket swing and spent many hours climbing in and out, flying to the stars and back.

Five decades later, I was surprised when I met one of my sister's classmates. She confessed that she was one of those curious children on the bus that "saw" the rocket launch. She asked me, after all these years, what the true story of the space launch was. I just smiled and answered, "Well, you saw the launch. All I can say is that rocket flew, and did contribute to learning and exploration, but definitely fell short of the moon!"

Chapter 13 – The Strikes

Throughout history, workers have rightfully, at times, protested wages, banded together with unions, and through a process of striking, or refusing to work, as a united group, gained greater wages. I am not going to get into the politics of strikes. I will just relate some of what it felt like as a child.

The first thing I think of when someone says the word "strike", is dinner of navy beans with no pork, or tomato sauce, just white navy beans, and boiled potatoes. I can picture making roads with our forks in our potatoes, "hauling" white boiled navy beans and "dumping" them with our forks in pretend stockpiles on our plates as we re-arranged them to make them more palatable before they were eaten. This was our dinner for many nights during strikes. It started out with navy beans with ham hock, ketchup for flavoring and boiled potatoes. When the ham hock was gone, and the ketchup was gone, we would just get white navy beans and boiled potatoes. We were far from starving. We still got oatmeal or cornmeal mush for breakfast and jelly sandwiches for lunch with peanut butter, until the peanut butter was gone. There was always plenty of jelly, because we had fruit trees.

We were pretty lucky. I only remember two strikes. The first strike was in 1956. I was young, and don't remember much except my mother and father worrying about bills, which ones to pay and which ones to wait on. That strike did not last very long.

The strike I remember the most was in 1960. It started in May and didn't end for about 220 days. It ended in early December.

School let out soon after the strike started. During the summer we could get along fairly inexpensively. One memory that summer was a slippery issue.

Butter was a commodity that seven children can consume fairly quickly. It is also not that inexpensive for a family that doesn't own a cow. My grandparents, living on the north fork of the Coeur d'Alene River, did own cows, however. My grandmother had an old milk Guernsey mix cow she regularly milked and old Shorthorn cow that had lost her calf. She was keeping the shorthorn milked out until she dried up. That left two people with two cows worth of milk and cream. She had plenty of neighbors to sell milk to, but, at that time, not as many places for the cream. That left our grandmother "swimming" in cream when our father paid a visit one afternoon.

Father arrived home that evening with five gallons of cream that needed to be dealt with right away before it spoiled. My mother was not too pleased. What was she to do with five gallons of cream? My father assured her he had been "studying the problem" on the way home. He also assured her he had things "well in hand".

He proceeded to the bathroom where our old wringer washing machine stood. Now, for anyone who doesn't know what an old wringer washing machine tub looks like, I should explain a few things. The most important thing is that a wringer washer is blessed with a large solid porcelain tub without "holes". What was about to take place could not have happened in an automatic washer, ventilated with holes. The old wringer washer also had a substantial agitator blade in the middle of the tub with "wings" on it, not like the modern automatic washers that just have a tube type agitator in the middle, or none at all.

Father thoroughly washed and rinsed the washing machine after pulling it out into the kitchen, amid protests from our mother. He poured all five gallons of cream into the washer, measured in the proper amount of salt and turned the washer on.

It took a while to work, as we stood around in awe, but eventually we had butter! We had to drain off the excess liquid and then pack the butter in large chunks rolled in wax paper and placed in bread bags. We froze the extra butter, to be used later.

The cleanup of the washing machine was not a job for the faint of heart, but we did have plenty of butter through the strike!

Fall was upon us and the strike had not ended. There were winter clothes to buy and there was no money. My father came home with news that the valley citizens had banded together and donated clothes that would be available in a church in Mullan, a small town about six miles to the east of Wallace. Most of our clothes were handed down, or purchased from the Montgomery Ward catalogue. We loaded up and went to the church to see what we could scavenge for school clothes. We were most in need of winter coats and boots. The smaller children could fit our hand-me downs, but children don't all grow the same, so sometimes this didn't work.

It was a humbling feeling, going through mounds of cast off clothing, looking for clothes that looked nice enough to wear to school. I still remember the varied smells of donated clothing, and feeling like I wasn't sure I wanted to try on something that smelled of strange unfamiliar scents. We all persisted, and came away with some really nice looking clothes. I remember my mother saying that we didn't have to tell kids at school where they came from if anyone made any comments. She advised us just to say they were hand-me downs from a sister or cousin. I remember practicing what I was going to say as I wore the clothes to school that fall.

I also remember that no one ever made any comments, and the subject never came up, which I was thankful for. I actually became very fond of a pair of boots I found in that pile, and a beautiful skirt. I think I wore them both out!

Although the strike ended in early December, it took forever to catch back up again on bills. It still affected Christmas greatly. We usually were allowed to "earn" some spending money for small gifts for everyone in the family. Not that Christmas. We were also told not to expect much. I remember my brother taking old wood and making a small rocking horse with my father's table saw for my youngest sister, Natalie. He also made a miniature cart and horse that pulled it with more scrap lumber my dad had got from a saw mill. I helped him by painting the picture of a silly horse on the side of the cart. I remember making foot tall cardboard paper dolls with paper clothes to dress them in. They were gifts for the younger children. Some of them were teddy bears and some were gingerbread men. Being of cardboard, and being larger they held up better for younger children to play with. Sissy made dresses for the younger girls. We expected little, that Christmas, and the little seemed like a lot. It was a happy Christmas, anyway, filled with a sense of accomplishment when the younger children's eyes lit up at our homemade gifts.

We all learned three great lessons from that strike. The first one is that the more you learn to do without, the less you have to have. The second one was that it does hurt to be humble, but it feels better after. The third is that there is always a place for something you can't use, and there is always someone with less than you have. I do appreciate those that gave during that strike.

Chapter 14 - Fire, Ice and Snow

Winter is cold and long in northern Idaho but can be full of magic and adventure for a child. Our father had the heart of a child. Our mother worried a lot. In the winter, when snow piled up, keeping the house warm and thinking of things to keep seven children from going stir crazy in a small one bathroom home built in 1910 were major concerns for two parents who saw the world a bit differently. During the week, my mother was saved by the fact that four of the seven were already in school while my father was at work. During the weekends, things got a little crazy, so when, on the rare occasion, my father was not working, he took charge of things. This meant ordering every one of us, small and large, to don our outdoor clothes, beginning with long underwear, double socks, outer pants, flannel shirts, then snow pants, coats, mittens, stocking hats, scarves, and out the door we tumbled. Our favorite time was when our father "got off" work on the 3:00 p.m. "shift". By the time he got home and had supper it was already dark and our mother was desperate for some alone time. Our father would head out with orders for us to all come along after the clothing ritual. By the time we arrived at the sledding hill, about 400 foot long tractor trail coming off a grade of about ten percent. It was a pretty good sized sledding hill. Father would build a huge bonfire in the middle of the bottom of the slope. The fire covered about three to four feet wide. The hill was about twenty feet wide, leaving about eight or nine feet of clearance on either side of the fire. There was plenty of room around either side of the fire, but it made the "run" a little more interesting, plus provided plenty of light to see where we were going. When the "little kids" got tired, they could sit by the fire and warm up, and we could roast marshmallows when we took a break. Mother would stand inside the house, and I'm afraid, wasted most of her alone time peering out the window to make sure no one landed in the fire!

Self preservation prevailed and none of us ever went up in smoke, but visions of those bonfires are forever imprinted in our memories.

On warmer snowy days, when all of us children ventured out alone, we invented a game that took advantage of the snow. We would break up into two teams. The teams consisted of the "running" team and the "tracking" team. The "running" team had a twenty minute head start. We would take off with at least one of the three "little children" in tow. Slogging through the snow….making huge footprints as we went, we would sneak up the mountain, or behind sheds, woodpiles, old cars, or piles of junk, seeking hiding spots, or ways to walk on bare ground to foil our "seekers". The hardest part was to keep the "little kids" from getting tired and squealing out, giving up our location. It helped to bring crackers and water or cut up apple for bribes.

We never allowed to go to the old mine tunnel behind the house during these adventures. This was Secret Hiding Place in the summer. The old mine sat during the winter, shrouded in ice and snow. The entrance held the stench of rotten clay-rock and decaying plants. It crouched, in wait with loose rocks to fall and timbers which might loosen and drop on any unwary man or animal that might venture inside. Just outside the tunnel, though, hung huge icicles, glistening in the midday sun like rainbows shining through crystals. These inviting icicles were an excellent water source for the tired snow child whether being pursued or as the pursuer. We would gently pluck the choice icicles as each child chose their own special one. A nearby bush on a small mound behind the garage provided a perfect hiding spot, where we would not easily be seen by the other team. There, the smaller children could rest and we could all enjoy our frozen, sparkling water as we planned the next leg of our journey.

The chasing game usually ended with the smallest members getting too cold or too much snow in their boots to go on. No matter how cold or tired we would all get, though, the next time the game was proposed, each of us was ready for a new adventure.

Our father pushing snow along our road across the crooked bridge in the winter

Chapter 15 – Winter Wonderland Wallace, Idaho

My husband and I come from the same small town of Wallace. As children, we agree on three special winter memories of our hometown.

Winter storms would signal snow forts and snowball fights on the playground at school. Large snowflakes would drift like goose down from a pillow. The snow would pile up on the streets of Wallace. In the evening, the drifting feathery snow appeared to land softly on white bed sheets piled in soft billowy clouds on the sides of the streets and sidewalks. As the street lamps came on in the early evening, the world was bathed in a soft yellow glow, with tiny ice crystals sparkling like stars in the night.

Christmas holiday scenes decorated the windows and toy departments in stores such as J.C. Penny's and Tabors, appearing before every Christmas like a "Santa's Workshop" dream for all the local children to gaze upon; each child hoping that one of those wondrous gifts would end up under their Christmas tree. Some "Santa" creations rarely seen by present day children were "three foot walking horses", twenty-nine inch walking dolls, wooden tinker toys, erector sets (making a comeback), metal "Tonka" trucks, graders, and tractors, "Easy-bake" ovens (also making a comeback), and electric trains set up complete with villages.

The star of the show was the lighted Christmas tree on King Street hill that was decorated yearly by the local power company in Wallace at the time. Decorations and lights were maintained yearly by the company.

The Tree on King Street Hill

The tree was lit every Christmas with care.

All the people in town were certain to be there.

The colors shone over the town so bright.

Little Wallace had a big tree that Christmas Eve night!

The feathery snow crunched under their feet,

As everyone gathered in the silent street.

Then down to the church for a Christmas Eve mass.

The lights were glowing through the church's stained glass.

The choir was singing carols of Christmas for all.

You could smell the incense as you entered the church hall.

I reached for some change to put in the box.

And out of my pocket pulled a bright sock!

Imagine my embarrassment as I looked up to see,

The priest, of all people, staring down at me!

Put that sock in your pocket, you dear little boy.

Then, put it over the fireplace, or you won't get a toy!

I heard him exclaim as he walked out of sight,

Christmas blessings to all, peace be with you and good night!

Eekraemer

Chapter 16 – A Topic of Many Points

When I got old enough to ask for a kitten, Mother explained that we could not keep a kitten. Animals drank water from the river, which ran grey with lead tailings from the mine. They also licked their paws, ingesting the lead from the tailings in the topsoil and eventually died from seizures. The same thing happened to our dogs. I remember a little spaniel when I was small. She was named Spotty, which was appropriate, since she was spotted black and white. She used to let me and my brother bury her, except for just her head, in the sand pile. She had mounds of patience. She died from seizures. We later learned that they were most likely caused from drinking the lead laced water in the grey river that ran by our home. When I was four years old, we went to a rancher who lived close to my grandmother on the North Fork of the Coeur d'Alene. I remember the rancher was called "Arizona Jack". I wasn't very old, but I remember that I was enamored by "cowboys" at that time. I thought this rancher was pretty awesome! He had cowboy boots, a cowboy hat, and actually carried a pistol on his hip! To top that off, he had an old female shepherd with a huge batch of puppies. I was told I could pick out a puppy. I immediately chose a little brown puppy that approached me and licked my hand. I quickly advised the mother dog that she didn't need to worry about that puppy because he wasn't her puppy any more, he was my puppy!

We taught our puppy not to go to or drink the water from the river. He learned quite fast, and he had no problems with seizures.

That puppy taught me a lot about love, responsibility and thoughtfulness. I still remember one day when I got in trouble. I was pouting in the back yard, feeling extremely sorry for myself. My dog came up to say he was sorry and licked my face. I didn't want anyone to tell me they were sorry! I wanted to pout! I pushed him away and screamed, "GO AWAY"! Then I kicked out at him. My mother witnessed the whole thing. She came out and scolded me and told me that all my little dog wanted to do was give me his love. She explained that he wanted to tell me how he cared about me. She shamed me and asked me how I could be so uncaring, mean and so selfish as to push that love away. She asked me if I could see how bad I now made him feel. Wow! That really hit home. I gave him a hug and apologized and asked him to forgive me. In the process, I totally forgot why I was feeling sorry for myself, but I never forgot how ashamed I felt for my actions or how willing my dog was to forgive me and be my friend again.

That little brown shepherd taught me another thing too. He taught me about death. That next winter he caught a cold. Water ran from his eyes, he coughed and yellow snot ran from his nose. He walked around with his head hanging and soon he didn't want to play or eat. I can remember my dad offering him the whole can of dog food. He just looked at it. We didn't have a local vet. People just didn't take their animals to veterinarians very often back then. The next day I looked for my dog. I found him lying where he had fallen. He was very stiff and still. He was lying in about two feet of snow, where he had fallen, in the still uncovered cement basement section of the addition my father had started for the new living room the fall before. He looked like he was sleeping, but I knew something was wrong, and he wouldn't wake up to my call. I got my mother. They wouldn't let me see him again. They said he had died of a sickness and we might catch it. I learned later that my dog had distemper. I was six years old at the time. We were not allowed to get another dog until I was fourteen years old. We got that dog vaccinations.

One day when I was about twelve years old, we got a surprise visitor. My father was working out in the front yard in the springtime. Out from under the porch wandered a porcupine as sedately as you please. Dad called all of us out of the house and advised us to keep our distance. We happened to have a big old wooden box about four feet high and three feet square. He and my brother drug the box over in front of the porcupine, who was now chewing on some fresh lilac sprouts. He then got a long plank and explained to us that he was going to catch the porcupine so that we could learn more about porcupines for a greater understanding.

He explained that porcupines do not "shoot" quills as is commonly thought, but that the quills have to actually be touched for them to imbed into the attacker. He showed us, by touching his quills with a board. Yes, indeed, when the board was withdrawn, it was loaded with quills! He then explained that porcupines are very vulnerable on their stomachs, which are soft and not covered with quills. He gently tipped the porcupine on its side so we could see the soft underside. He also explained that over all, porcupines have a very docile nature. He then had my brother take another long plank, and between the two of them, they herded the porcupine into the box. The box was then tipped upright, and we had a porcupine for a pet!

He put hay in the bottom of the box and gently lowered water that we could fill with a watering can. We fed him apples, carrots and fresh willow twigs. When we went to bed that night, we were all excited to have a new, strange pet. Just studying him that evening, he seemed not a bit aggressive. He just sat looking back at us, nibbling on the apples we had given him. My brothers and sisters and I started making plans as to how we were going to fashion a leash to take him for walks.

The next morning, our father awoke us early. He announced that we needed to turn the porcupine loose "right away", even before breakfast. It seems he had been thinking that night. Early in the morning he awoke and turned the porcupine on its side again, just enough to confirm his suspicions. Mr. Porcupine was a Mrs. Porcupine. She was starting to leak some milk, and either was about to have some little porcupettes or had just given birth recently to some. We all agreed that it was time for the porcupine to go home as quickly as possible. We carried the box over to the edge of the forest. We tipped the box on its side so the porcupine could walk out to freedom. She calmly ambled out of the box and up the mountain without as much as a wiggle of her tail.

Many years later, I asked my father if he really thought the porcupine had her babies in the forest already. He said that she appeared to be quite a chubby porcupine for one that was nursing young ones, and it didn't appear that she had been suckled on. He figured that she was probably just about to give birth. He said he figured that she was snooping around the old porch for a place to give birth. He said that although it might have been nice for us to see some baby porcupettes, (young porcupines), their quills only stay soft for a couple of days. He said he didn't care to pull quills out of children's hands that might want to hold cute little porcupettes.

Chapter 17 - The Wild Ones

It was only natural that we would occasionally have wild animals around our place. We lived between a mountain and a river. You just never knew what kind of animal would show up on the doorstep.

There was Sammy the flying squirrel that got caught in our chimney. It happened on a day when our father wasn't home. Evidently he had soared out of a tree on the hillside and landed on the top of our chimney and slipped in. Fortunately for the squirrel, it was a chimney for a stove in the basement that we rarely used. There was a hole in the chimney on the main floor of the house where a stove could be hooked up, but just had a plate over it. We heard a terrible scratching and screeching coming from our chimney, close to the plate hole, on the main floor. My mother was expecting a mouse or wood rat, but she was more afraid it was a bat. She donned a pair of my father's very heavy leather welding gloves and had us slowly open the plate on the chimney. As the squirrel stuck his head out, mother grabbed him and hung on for dear life. He was young and just as surprised as we were. His dark eyes seemed huge. Flying squirrels are nocturnal, so it was probably hard for him to see us well in the bright lights of the house. Mother took him outdoors and, before she set him loose, showed us his skin stretched between his feet for wings. It was fascinating to get a first-hand look at a rather rare little creature. She took him to the old cedar tree on the hillside and turned him loose.

One afternoon, my mother came running into the house, out of breath, face as white as a cornstarch. She had a broom in her hand. It was mid-summer, she had been outdoors hanging up cloths on the line when, at a side glance, she thought she saw a large Labrador dog, tongue hanging out running across the side yard to the pond by the old mine tunnel. She went to the porch and grabbed a broom to chase him off. She went for him saying "Shoo! Shoo! Get out of here, you…" She never got any further with her shooing, I guess. At that point, she was almost on top of him. He turned and she realized it wasn't a large dog at all, but a young black bear!! Mom ran one way, the bear ran the other.

Young yearling bears were common. Some young bears hung around more than others. Usually they were just curious and liked to fill their stomachs at our old apple tree in the back yard.

One year, an especially curious young black bear decided to check out our porch. That was just a little too close for comfort! We were also scared for our new collie pup that was sleeping in a cardboard box with a hole cut in the front for her to crawl in. My father was working night shift, or "graveyard", as it was called. We could hear him clawing and snuffling at the door. My mother screamed and hollered at him and pounded on pots and pans. He finally left. We children were crying because we supposed the bear ate the puppy. She was fine, crouched in the back corner of the little cardboard box. There were scratches on the door where the bear had tried to gain entrance. The next night, the bear again returned and tried to get in the house. Our father was home, and would have none of that nonsense! We had bear steaks the next night. Actually, they were pretty good.

Another memorable visitor was also discovered by our mother. She was walking across our bridge to get the paper on the other side. Guess she was thinking hard about something, because she was in the middle of the bridge before she realized there was someone else on the bridge, crossing on the edge, about three feet from her. Basically, they were almost face to face. It was a young cougar. She had the presence of mind to let out a large shout. The cougar must have realized he wasn't welcome. He zipped past her and up the mountain. We never saw him again.

Other animals that had a part-time home with us were a young bear cub that spent the summer and eventually grew large enough to leave. He returned in the spring with another young bear, still small and stunted. He hung around for a while, but never caused any trouble. He eventually wandered off and never returned. There was also a young elk that left with the herd once he had regained his strength.

Our father remained stern on the fact that nature cares for its own in strange ways, and although we can lend aid, we don't want to keep anything from its natural life for long.

Elk and deer frequented our place in the winter when the snows were deep up above and in the early fall before hunting season. I think sometimes that animals that are hunted must be able to read the news. They always seem to know when hunting season approaches. The smart ones seem to disappear to their favorite spots where they can watch hunters desperately trying to fathom their whereabouts.

Babe was the most lasting of our wild visitors. I don't know if you could really classify him as wild. He was a golden mantled ground squirrel. Most people just call them chipmunks, but they are really different. A chipmunk is tiny, fox faced and extremely quick in his movements. A golden mantled ground squirrel is striped like a chipmunk, but larger and basically just has a more rounded look. He is also quick, but not jerky in his movements, and is definitely braver.

Our father had been working with his loader, removing dirt from the hillside to put on the road. He had stopped to come in for lunch. We children were all outdoors playing when we heard small squeaks coming from the dirt in the pile our father had just dumped. We set to digging with our hands. Not far under the soil, under a tree branch was a tiny rock squirrel baby. He was a mess with soil sticking out of his mouth. We took him in the house, washed his mouth out, cleaned him up and put him on a hot water bottle wrapped in a towel in an old bird cage. We fed him regular cow's milk heated and he drank out of a doll's bottle. Probably what saved him was that he was only about a week away from weaning, yet still young enough not to be really afraid. You wouldn't think something as small as a squirrel could be smart, but that little rock squirrel was really smart. Our cousin had just got married. He and his wife lived in a trailer and had no pets. When they came to visit, they fell in love with Babe and took him home with them. They kept him in their trailer where they would let him out to play. He came to know he had to go back into his cage if they left, or if it was bed time. He even got out of their trailer a few times, but came back in when he was called. The next year, when Babe was full grown, our cousin and his wife decided it was time for Babe to have his freedom. They brought him back to the house. We took him out in the back yard and turned him loose. He stayed pretty close for the first few days, and then slowly drifted off to do what rock squirrels do. He would still come to us when we called, though. If we had food for him, we just had to call him by name and he would show up, climb up, and sit on our hand. I should mention that we could tell him from other rock squirrels not only because he was tame, but because he had stuck his nose through the cage so many times when he was little that he made a mark on his nose that stayed permanently. That fall, Babe was around a bit later than the other rock squirrels or chipmunks. We worried he wouldn't know how to hibernate. Eventually he disappeared. All the long winter we wondered if he would show up again in the spring. The next spring as the snow melted and the streams ran full and the sun warmed the rocks and the trilliums bloomed, the first chirps of chipmunks and squirrels were heard. We ran for our treats to see if Babe would appear. We didn't have to wait long! Babe did appear. He was sassier than ever! He would still climb up our pants and sit on our shoulder, but didn't stay as long. He had a girlfriend too! Later that summer, the young squirrels came out. There was Babe. Then, to our surprise, we weren't feeding one squirrel; we were feeding his children too! Babe was teaching his children to come to our call and eat out of our hand! Year after year, Babe returned. One time he showed up with a hurt foot. One time he had deep scratches on his back. For six years Babe returned and brought his children for us to feed. I guess you would say our place became a golden mantled ground squirrel preserve, of sorts.

Chapter 18 - The Checkerboard Bus

It is not easy to go places with nine people, even before the seat belt law. In the early 1960s, it was getting increasingly difficult for our parents to safely afford transportation for the whole family in one vehicle.

My father came up with a quite an inventive idea when he brought home an old hearse from a local funeral home. He explained to our less than enthusiastic mother that he had acquired it from the local car lot for a real steal. The hearse ran like a dream and was extremely roomy inside. The back end where we larger kids were to sit was lined of very soft velvet. We were all eager to take some exciting trips in our shiny black caravan! There was one interesting thing about this new acquisition. The inside of it smelled anything but new. Father said it would just take time for the strange smell to dissipate. My sister, who was taking biology in high school at the time, swore the smell was of formaldehyde. My father got a funny look on his face when the subject arose at the dinner table. My mother refused to visit her family in a hearse. My father took the hearse down to the local car dealer the next day.

Sitting on the car lot, ripe for a trade-in was a yellow school bus. Needless to say, by the end of the day, we were the proud owners of a slightly used, but pretty awesome yellow and black school bus. Now, so you get the right picture, our father didn't get carried away about this. It was the shorter model, not the big long one that carries a "zillion" students. This one could only hold about 30 or so. Mother wasn't sure what to think when we came home with the school bus, but she was so glad not to see the hearse she didn't say much.

Dad sweetened the pot by promising to "deck" the bus out with amenities. He did this in short order. He made bunk beds in the back, taking out three rows of seats and replacing them with a two by four frame with plywood to hold the mattresses and two full sized mattresses as bunks. This was great for letting the little ones nap, or a place to read while we drove down the road. In the mid-section he took out one set of seats on the left side and turned one set around. In the section where one set of seats were, he put a table in that folded down against the wall when it wasn't in use. It rarely got folded down. The bars up by the driver were great exercise bars for the "little kids" when we made longer trips. I guess it's a good thing there were no safety belt laws back then! We took some wonderful family trips in that old school bus! The other great thing about the bus was that all of the children that regularly got car sick on the way to visit family in Sandpoint (myself included), no longer got car sick! That clinched it for our mother. She was in love with that bus! One annoying thing, however, about this bus was that every time we went to Coeur d'Alene or Sandpoint, we got pulled over by the State Police! It seems that they had to check out any school buses loaded with children that looked suspicious since some unwary driver just might want to make off with some innocent school children and take them to Mexico or the salt mines of Bulgaria. About the sixth time this happened, my father had an extra long talk with the State Trooper. He seemed a friendly sort and all too willing to assist my father with a plan to end this continual interchange. It seems they only targeted school buses that were the original color. Although, at the time, there was no law to require he change the color of the bus,(a law was later put into effect to require private owners to change the color of their buses), my father decided it was time to end this exchange for once and for all. He stopped at a local convenience store and purchased two spray cans of forest green paint. At the side of the road, halfway between Coeur d'Alene and Sandpoint, our bus went from being a standard short yellow school bus to a green and yellow checkerboard bus! In 1960, we went south to see Boise, Idaho and the Capitol building. In 1962 we went to see the Seattle World's fair. The bus behaved itself like a champion. It even managed to work in a few quiet hours on a Washington beach wiggling its four tires in the sand. We met our cousins in Seattle and had a crazy but memorable tour of the World's Fair and Space Needle. With both families, we totaled seventeen, (four adults and 13 children between the ages of 17 and 4 months. They all fit in the bus. We even managed a birthday party complete with cake for my young cousin's seventh birthday while we were driving over the newly opened Evergreen, floating bridge. I remember my father and uncle explaining floating bridges to us, and how the bridge, itself did not exactly float on top of the water but that the bridge was set on piers anchored to large floating concrete pontoons, (each about the size of a football field), which were in turn, anchored to the lake bottom.

In the summer when we weren't going anywhere, the bus sat in the front yard and we children slept in it, camping out and talking till all hours of the night. It seems the local Forest Service liked the green on the bus, because after the checkerboard paint job they called my father to see if it could be put on the list for transporting fire fighters during the fire seasons. I really don't remember if it ever was used, but we were extremely proud of our bus that it could serve in such a capacity.

The checkerboard bus was an honored member of our family. The places we were able to travel together gave our family of nine, a convenience, a sense of freedom and a chance for learning that we never would have had during those times without that checkerboard bus.

Chapter 19 - The "Duck"

A duck, an army duck, that is, is a six wheeled amphibious vehicle that, as amphibious would lead you to guess, travels both on land and on water. General Motors created the DUKW or duck for the army during World War II to transport goods over land and water and for landing on beaches during attacks.

DUKW stood for: D for a design from 1942; U for utility; K meant "all wheel drive"; and W indicated two powered rear axles.

The duck or "Magoo", another nickname given by the army, weighed 7.5 tons and drove down the road at no more than 55 miles per hour. Its top speed on water was about 6.4 miles per hour. It was 8.25 feet wide and 8.8 feet high with a canvas top that folded up. It was a whole thirty-one feet long, with tires that dwarfed me at five foot two inches. Only 21,137 were manufactured between about 1945 and 1950. Most ducks were decommissioned and sold as surplus after World War II. They are still used now by some communities for flood rescue.

The duck is actually the first vehicle made that allowed the driver to vary the tire pressure from inside the cab. Afterward, General Motors used the same technology on the army Humvee.

My father was always coming up with ideas on how he could move earth, move buildings, build things, or tear buildings down, depending upon the extra job he hired on for in addition to his regular job at one of the local mills in the valley. These ideas usually would lead to a need for him to acquire a new piece of equipment which would be added to his growing collection. A brand new piece of equipment was out of the question. The cost of a large piece of road equipment is not for the faint of heart. My father would spend many hours making his case to my mother about the cost effectiveness of his proposed new piece of equipment before he went out on the "purchasing trail". He always won. Now, you have to remember, there were no computers, or "seller's listings" at your fingertips, no on-line bidding.

Our father would set forth reading all the newspaper ads and inquiring of equipment sales places within a two hundred mile radius.

The spring that I graduated from high school I was seventeen years old. My father graduated, also, to surplus equipment auctions. He needed bigger equipment in the form of a truck shovel. A truck shovel was listed at an auction that spring and my father was bent on acquiring it. My brother was no longer living at home, so my sister and I went as backup so someone could drive his pickup home if he bought anything. The auction was long and boring. It was long and boring even when my father beat out one other bidder and got his truck shovel for what he deemed a "bargain price". I'm thinking he was serious about the "bargain price", because of what happened next. The next vehicle out was Mr. Duck, "yep", the "Magoo". It was an amphibious vehicle, looking like a huge ugly camouflaged hippo. No one bid. My father, getting ready to go, turned back around. Thought a minute, and raised his hand! You have to be kidding me! What did he think he was doing! Mother was going to just kill him! Four bids later, my father was the proud owner of the most monstrous looking "animal-ishly" clumsy vehicle I had ever seen.

After paying for the obscenity and the sweet, but large bright orange truck shovel, my father walked up to my sister and me and changed our lives. "Now here's the thing", he began. I knew we were in for trouble when he started out like that! "I can leave the pickup here because it is parked out on the street, but...." Now, I truly knew we were in for it. "I need to get both the truck shovel and the duck home at once. They need the lot clear." Those words echoed in my ears, and bounced around in my head for a couple of seconds. Then I realized he was still talking. "You two are going to have to drive the duck home." I, being the oldest, had the driver's license, but, I was the faint of heart. I was the child that found it comfortable to just step back into the crowd of children in the family. Where was that crowd now? My sister, at 14 could drive but didn't have her license yet. She was excited and eager. I could hear her beside my father. "Drive the duck! Yeah, sure, cool!" I was thinking, "Yeah, sure, cool, my eye!" "Was she crazy?" My sister was taller than I. She was actually normal height at about 5 foot 4 inches. She was also more self assured. I got the shorter end by a full two inches, and didn't see any point at being self assured. Right away I explained to my father that I thought we would do far better with the truck shovel. It had an actual cab, even if it was off to one side and even if there was a large shovel attached on the back. My father would have none of it. He explained that although the tires were almost taller than I, that once we got inside we would see that there was far better view in the Duck and it would be easy to steer down the road. I had some doubts about that. He explained that the truck shovel was extra wide, but that cars probably would not give it as wide a berth, and I would probably take out a car or two on the way home. In contrast, cars would see the duck and be all too willing to give me plenty of room.

My sister and I climbed aboard. There was actually a ladder on the side. After we climbed in, our father explained the gear set up and what to touch and not to touch. I can remember him saying above all, not to touch the deflator for the tires. It was set for road travel. You could deflate them if you were in sand or mud. That probably wouldn't work too well for the freeway. The Duck started amazingly easy. I was shaking so bad, it was a good thing the steering was really stiff. My sister and I worked it out that she would shift and I would drive. After getting everything sorted out I felt a tad more confident. The old competitive spirit had also taken hold. I couldn't let my younger sister know just how scared I really was! I know I said that ducks could go as fast as fifty-five miles per hour, but I'll bet we clocked along at about thirty-five for at least the first few miles. I could say that all went perfect, and that was that, but for one catch. As we were trundling along, I noticed that my father, (who was following us in the truck shovel), kept getting closer and closer with the large truck shovel. I thought he meant that I was probably going too slowly, so I kept inching a little faster and then a little bit faster. He would then inch closer again. Finally it became clear he wanted us to pull over when he started flashing his lights. I found a wider spot and pulled over, thankful for the chance to stop, but fearful of what I was doing wrong. Did I unwittingly run over something? All sorts of scenarios were filling my head. My father was laughing when he came up to the side of the duck. The duck had evidently been out for a swim with its prior owners and they had left the propeller engaged. I learned that, like checking for an emergency brake to be on, with a duck, you need to check to make sure the propeller is disengaged! In all, we only had about ten miles to cover to get the duck home. That was the longest ten miles of my life. We did it, though! We did not drive across that crooked bridge. Our father did. Yes, it held up just fine, but, I think he figured he had tested my perseverance enough for one day.

The duck found a place in our hearts and in our father's odd collection of vehicles. The story might end there, or it might end with my father's plan to take it up to Sandpoint, Idaho, my mother's hometown to Lake Pend Oreille and take us all out on the lake in it. The duck, however, was destined for a different ending. The first part of the story I know for a fact. The second part of the story is just something I heard, but I can't tell you if it is so or not. A gentleman, driving by on the road one day stopped and asked my father if the duck was for sale. Dad was working many hours and didn't have a lot of time for leisure those days. Money was scarce once again, and I suppose he figured the duck was like money in the bank that needed withdrawing. He gave the man a price and the duck was sold. He went through the workings of the duck it with him, showing him how everything worked. The last thing he said to him as he drove away was, "And, don't forget to make sure the plugs are in if you take it out on the water!" A few years later my father said he heard that the man did just what my dad had planned on. Supposedly he took the Duck up to Lake Pend Oreille and put it in for a leisurely voyage. Only, he forgot to put the plugs in. The story is that Mr. Duck may still lie at the bottom of Pend Oreille Lake.

Above, is a picture of Bayview, Idaho, on Pend Oreille Lake, (originally named Lake Kalispell), the largest and deepest lake in Idaho. This is where Farragut Naval Training Station was built in 1942 for Naval submarine training. It also served as a prisoner of war camp during World War II. The training station closed in 1946, but continued on as Farragut College and Technical Institute until 1949. Around 2,500 acres of the area became Farragut State Park in 1964.

Chapter 20 – "It Stinks"

First of all, I want to make it clear that I do not believe the South Fork of the Coeur d'Alene, River presently "stinks".

I was born in the Providence Hospital, Wallace, Idaho, 1948. I was brought home from the hospital to the same home I left to get married twenty-one years later. I climbed over the mountains behind our home, and I made foot tracks in the gray sand by the side of the gray river that ran by our home. I sat under the yellow moon by the side of the river and dreamed of the prince that was to sweep me off my feet and sail me away down that very gray river that was nicknamed "Lead Creek", but showed on the maps, even then, as the South Fork of the Coeur d'Alene River.

I was proud of our home, and my mother was extremely particular about our appearance, making sure we always went to school neat and clean. When our extended family came from out of town, I was proud to show them around. Part of the ritual in the summer was to take the cousins up on the mountain and sneak them for a walk down by the river. We weren't allowed down by the river, which made it all the more exciting of a tour!

Never did it enter my mind that our river might smell like sewage and mine waste.

The summer after I graduated from high school, I had agreed to counsel at a YMCA camp in Hamilton, Montana. It was only for a week, but this was a really big deal for me. I had never been gone for even one night away from all members of my family! I had spent three days at a time in Sandpoint, Idaho with my sister and brother in our cabin, but this was different!

Usually, our history teacher only chose juniors for counselors. I later learned that he chose me because I was immature and inexperienced for being a graduating senior, and he thought this might be a great way for me to get some experience out in the world. I was also young for a senior, and would not turn eighteen until that fall.

When he first asked me if I would like the job, I told him that I would love to, but because I was still seventeen, I would have to obtain my parent's permission. He said that was not a problem. He planned to stop by and talk to my parents. Personally, I thought he was going to hit a "dead end". I knew how far Jehovah's Witnesses made it when they came knocking on our door. My father was usually very nice and entertaining, but steadfast in his own ideas. No, the YMCA wouldn't make it past the door.

To my surprise, not only did my teacher get in the door, my mother offered him coffee and cookies. Father not only gave his consent, they talked for about an hour about life.

Hamilton is in southwestern Montana in the heart of the beautiful Bitterroot valley. It sits at the base of a mountain range that rises over 7,000 feet towards the sky. The camp was on the edge of a mountain lake. I couldn't have asked for a more heavenly job. The job as counselor turned into yet another job with a Girl Scout camp in the same location that summer. I was then offered another job as assistant cook, but by that time, I was so homesick I couldn't eat.

My teacher drove me in to the town of Hamilton and put me on a Greyhound bus headed back to Wallace and home.

By the time the bus was headed up Lookout Pass, (the pass that divides Montana from Idaho on I-90), I was so excited I could hardly sit still. Then, I started listening to the other passengers. Were they "nuts"? One lady was so scared, she hid her face. Another passenger asked if she had ever been in the mountains before. The lady's husband replied that she had not. They both had been raised on the plains of Ohio. Another passenger from the mid west chimed in and said she felt like the mountains were just going to fall in on us. I was amazed! I had exactly the opposite feeling. I was feeling secure, wrapped in the palm of the mountain's hand. All was well. My stomach and head were feeling better than they had for days!

When we came over the top of the mountain and headed down past Mullan, Idaho, my excitement was almost too much to contain. I was almost home! Just wait until this bus full of people saw how beautiful our little town was! They would forget about being scared about the mountains. To my surprise, as we came into Wallace, they started complaining about something else. "What is that horrible stench?" one lady exclaimed. Then, several more passengers chimed in with agreement. I was embarrassed and horrified. The awful thing was, then, that I, too, for the first time in my life, smelled what they smelled. What had happened to my dear home town? By the time I reached home, I realized the awful truth. Before the cleanup of the 1970's, our dear river, the South Fork of the Coeur d' Alenes, not only was grey, it had a definite stench! I had grown up accepting that in the middle of the winter, when the fog came in, we would also get the smell from the Bunker Hill Smelter. Some mornings when we walked to catch our bus, we would put our scarves over our noses to keep the smell out. It was an acrid, acidy smell, one that would burn your throat when it was too thick. You could taste a metallic taste in your mouth too. I hated to go to Kellogg during days like that, because the smell was a lot worse there. This was the first time, though, that I realized that Wallace generated a smell of its own! Well, I guess no one is perfect!

I now stand on the new bridge that goes to our family home. The river runs clean, fish and frogs thrive, and the air is heavy with the spring scents of wild honeysuckle and syringas blooming on the mountainside.

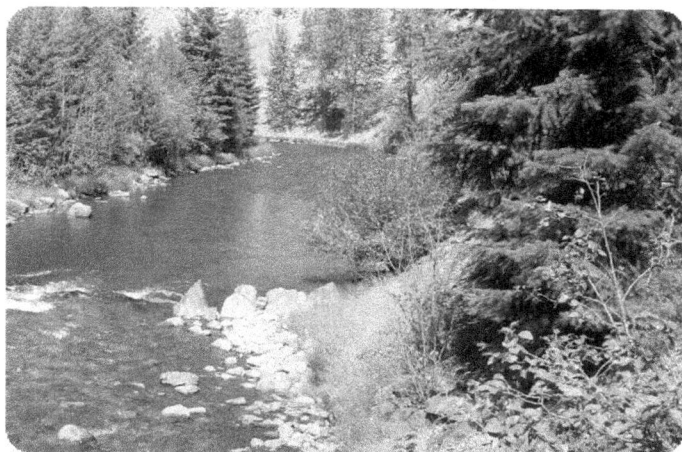

The South Fork of the Coeur d'Alene River near Where the Crooked Bridge Crossed

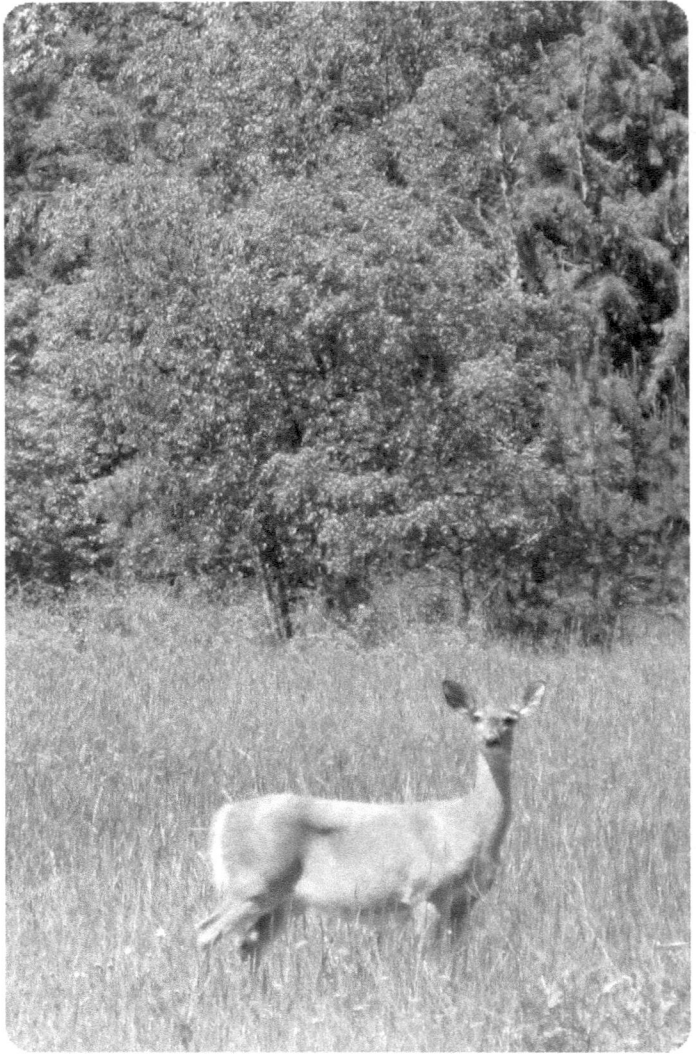

Chapter 21 - A Grand Old One

The fall after I graduated from high school, I didn't have enough money to start college, so I got a job working at the local newspaper. I typed the local news on a machine called a "teletype-setter". It looked like a large typewriter, but typed out a tape with punch holes, similar to Morse code. Each set of punch holes was equal to a letter in the alphabet. There was also an arrangement of punch holes that meant a space. There were two spaces; an 'n' space for the equal to one space and an 'm' space, equal to two spaces. There were no computers in those days to figure how to make the lines all equal on both sides and look uniform without too many spaces between words. People take for granted how columns of words are made to look even in newspapers, but even today, a computer is figuring how to space the words to keep it all even. I eventually figured out how to 'guess' as I went along to accomplish this as I typed. It became automatic to place 'm' spaces and 'n' spaces occasionally as I typed. After I had a large enough tape, or at the end of a page or article, I could tear the tape off and take the roll into the "typesetter". The 'typesetter' worked in the back room on a very large machine that had metal letters than came down on a line and was laid in a metal form when he typed. These were large letters for ad layouts. When the metal form was filled, he would pour hot lead into the form. When it set up, he could dump the lead out, pull out the letters and you would have a lead version of the advertisement. He could then set this lead version of the ad in a larger form where all the lead versions of all the ads would make up the page to a paper. Ink was spread over the lead form and the presses rolled over this lead form with lead type. The finished version was a newspaper advertisement. My spools went on the same machine where smaller type followed the same process, being guided by the holes in the tape as to which letters went into the small print form. The process was really fascinating. The typesetter machine and the 'teletype-setter' are now in history museums. The press, I am sure, went to the junk yard with the arrival of computers and offset printing.

When I first applied for the job, I was scared stiff! I had no idea what I was doing, or what to say. However, I was determined to convince the editor I could accomplish the job. I had taken two years of typing in school. I could somewhat proficiently type at sixty words per minute, but I had the habit of making more mistakes the more nervous I was. When asked how fast I could type, I confidently said "Sixty words per minute!" Well, that cinched it! (I could type sixty words per minute. He just didn't ask how many mistakes I made!) Typing at sixty words per minute was good enough to get the job. Two weeks later, the editor came to me and said that maybe I stretched my abilities a bit. Maybe if I didn't start producing a little faster, maybe I wouldn't have a job! Now, that scared me too much to be nervous any more. I determined to be the best and quickest copy typist ever hired. I resolved that if I got nervous and made mistakes, then, I would just have to type faster. The great thing about it was that erasing was easy. No erasing, no white-out, I just backed the tape up, marked out (which was equal to punching full holes across the tape), and re-typed faster than ever. I kept at it and doubled my time. My plan must have worked. The editor never complained about my work again. As time went on, I was somewhat promoted by being given additional duties. When the type editor was ill, I got to help fill in with type editing. I also was occasionally given the job of 'editing' the rest of the paper when the editor had a meeting to go to in the afternoon. He would tell me to find appropriate articles to fill in the rest of the paper of the Associated Press feed, or ad in local pieces where appropriate. Occasionally, I was asked to report on an event in the evening. At those times, I was also given the press camera to take pictures.

One weekend, in the late fall of 1968, my younger sister, and I were helping my father, who had been contracted to tear down a large portion of Hercules Mill, excepting the buildings that flanked the mill, including the central warehouse, assay office and some storage buildings. The Hercules Mill was a prominent structure that used to lie just west of Wallace, Idaho on the north hillside. It was built in 1912 and ran until 1940.

Below is a picture of my father moving the ball mill (a large rock grinder from the mill that tumbled metal balls inside it to crush ore) from the Hercules Mill. He used the power of the tractor to pull the two large trucks to haul the ball mill.

Our father had been working on the structure for a few months and had salvaged all he could. He started a section on fire to complete the demolition of the part of the mill he was contracted to remove. The fire burned much hotter than anticipated. My sister and I and our father hooked up an old fire hose he kept handy. I still remember the extreme power of that fire hose when the water came gushing out. I also remember the incredible force of those flames as we fought them back with the fire hose. I developed a keen respect for firefighters at that moment. We managed to get the fire under control before the fire engines arrived. The firemen stayed and watched; thus making sure the forest above didn't get involved. We were extremely fortunate. The fire went as planned, not burning any structures that were not intended for demolition.

The fire, itself was quite dramatic. It was probably one of the most exciting things that happened in that small town of Wallace for at least that year! The old mill boards were dry and burned fast. When the fire was no longer a danger, but still licking great flames high into the air, I ran to the truck and grabbed my trusty Kodak Instamatic camera. I snapped a few pictures. I gave my boss, the editor of the local paper some of the photos and negatives and a short summary of the happenings. I was thrilled that to find that the picture I took was on the front page!

On the following pages are a few of the pictures out of my scrapbook from that eventful day.

Hercules Mill July 1968 – Demolition Had Started

Demolition Fire .....

After the demolition, some buildings were left at the mill site.

2011 Picture of the Hercules Mill Site

The trees are restoring their claim.

Chapter 22 – Timothy and the Message

Our father was a child of the great depression and of divorce. He spent his childhood, from twelve years old to adulthood traveling between his mother and his father at will, hopping freight trains and listening to stories by the fireside under railroad bridges with transients and hobos. I guess you could say he was a self made man. You have to remember, though, this was in the 1930s. This is something I wouldn't recommend for a child of twelve today.

Father was hard working, a man of principles, a strict father, a doting husband, and a strong advocate of charity for the lost souls and 'underdogs' of this world. Many were the times we would stop along the roadside to pick up a hitchhiking stranger, or help someone with a broken down vehicle. Many were the times my father would pull out of his pocket a couple of dollars to help the wanderer on his way at the end of the ride.

Our father had the habit of either loaning or giving us at least our first car. "Sam", a blue Ford Fairlane was my first car. "Sam" was pretty, but a little tough to drive for a five foot two female. I had to put a small pillow under me on the seat to see properly. I lost "Sam" one day when my sister and her husband visited. They were having car problems which my father solved for them by giving them "Sam". I was really upset when that happened. I knew "Sam" was only loaned to me, but I had no idea how I was going to get to work the next morning unless I walked. It was about two miles in to work. It was do-able, but not something I would like to do every day. My father explained that he didn't see any problem, because I could just drive his recent acquisition. I didn't think much of my father's "recent acquisition." It was a 1953 Cadillac (this was around Christmastime, 1966, so actually, he was only thirteen model years old). He looked like an attempt at a civilian tank. He was black on the top and grayish white on the bottom. His interior was like a bad dream with bright red dashboard and bright blue seats with shiny threads that ran through the fabric. "I wouldn't, no couldn't be caught dead driving that thing!" Well, they say the word 'can't' "never solved anything." I did drive that car. Timothy was my second car. He was officially only borrowed from my dad, but mine at heart. I don't know why, but our family always named their cars. I do feel that cars develop personalities from the people operating them. Some of their personalities come from the people that designed or built them. When I get a car, the name comes from the later. Timothy was definitely a male. Timothy was big, tough and rugged, but with an elegant side, also. He had a deep roar in his engine, making him definitely male.

I was scared stiff when I took off to work in him the next morning. His hood was high and I was short. I had to double the pillow underneath me and practice stretching to hit the pedals. Maybe it made me taller, in all, however, because I eventually did grow an inch!

I learned to love that old "blunder bust"! Timothy had a V8 engine. He not only had power, he had weight. When the snows fell, Timothy plowed right through. When Dana and I made a weekend trip to Coeur d'Alene to shop all day in March, it began lightly sprinkling by early afternoon. By evening, it was pouring rain. We weren't worried about weather. Weather was the last thing on our minds. It was the weekend. It was spring! We were two young girls with a world to explore. Dana and I stayed in Coeur d'Alene past dark to eat out. To get home, we had to go over a mountain pass, the Fourth of July Canyon. Fourth of July Canyon can be treacherous in the winter. It can be warm and rainy in Spokane, Washington and Coeur d'Alene, Idaho, but go north, south, east or west and you hit the mountains and the ice and snow. This spring day that was exactly the case.

We headed home giggling and gabbing, radio blaring. When we hit the first turn on the pass we knew we were in trouble. The rain had turned to thick snow and the roadway had turned to solid ice. We lumbered past cars in the ditch, cars turned around going the wrong way, police lights flashing. We just kept going. My speed had dropped enormously. My foot was frozen on the pedal, trying to keep an even speed, yet keep climbing the steep mountain. A car slid in front of me and I hit the pedal going around and spun out on the next corner. Now, I was in the ditch headed the wrong way. A police car passed, lights flashing. He just kept going! I sat frozen a few minutes, and then pushed on, plowing my way out of the ditch with the sheer power of the car, flipping back around and proceeded up the mountain. I truly fell in love with that car in that moment! We persisted through one of the largest snowstorms of the season and arrived home without a scratch on person or car.

The next summer, Dana and I were once again heading in towards Coeur d'Alene on a weekend jaunt. We were as far as Cataldo when I saw a car parked on the side of the freeway. A lady and a man were outside the car looking like they didn't know what to do next. My sister and I pulled over. Now, you have to understand, that this was the 1960's. People in Idaho didn't worry about getting robbed or abducted or killed in turn for helping people in distress. We were just doing what our father would have done. We got out and asked if we could help. They explained that they were on their way to Spokane, Washington and were

104

out of gas and had no money. We explained that we were not far from the Cataldo exit and that (at that time) there was a service station in Cataldo where we could get some gas. We loaded the couple up in the car and drove them to the station. I gave him two dollars in cash, (which, at that time was plenty to get to Spokane, Washington). The filling station attendant loaned us a gas can, which he filled with the gas. We took them back to their car, helped them fill their car and start it, by priming it with a little gas in the engine. We went to leave, when the man called us back to his car. He opened up the back trunk. He explained that he wanted to give me something in turn for being kind. There in the back of the trunk lay a trillion boxes of jewelry! I never asked why he would be traveling with so many boxes of jewelry strewed about in his trunk, and he certainly never explained. He just reached in and handed me one of the boxes. I took it in dismay and thanked him. Later, I looked at the necklace. It was a beautiful pure silver heart, with hands folded in prayer. The sign, of Alpha and Omega, for the beginning and the end were engraved on the front. On the back was printed this simple verse:

"God grant me the serenity to accept the things I cannot change, the courage to change the things I can, and the wisdom to know the difference."   **Reinhold Niebuhr**

This simple, but powerful message has walked me through a lot of tough times in life. Each time I read it, hear it, or think about it, I can't help but remember that day on the road.

Timothy ended his life at almost that very spot that fall. My sister, Dana, and I were making another of our runs, this time, with the intent of going to Spokane, Washington. It was a beautiful fall day. Timothy was zooming along, the radio was blaring. All of a sudden he let out a high pitched squeal and started clunking loudly. I pulled over on the side of the interstate, only yards from where the people were stopped. Timothy never ran again. He had lost his rear end! We called our father from the same service station that we got the gas for the people. Our father came out and towed Timothy home.

R.I.P. Timothy. He spent his final days on the hillside, under the pine trees. I always planned to get him fixed, but life happens, marriage, and children. When I finally got the money together to fix Timothy up he was literally melting back into the ground. He had found his resting place. I settled for one hubcap for memory.

Chapter 23 - A Sticky Problem

A trip to town with our father was not a common occurrence. We treasured these times. One spring day when I was about ten years old, my brother, Jimmy, older sister, Lana, my younger sister, Dana and I went with my father downtown to purchase birthday gifts for our little sister, Kate. We children had a grand plan to have a real birthday party for her two year old birthday. We saved up our junking money and had plans to purchase balloons and candles along with the gifts we could afford. Small change went a lot further in those days, so, when I lost a quarter down the grate in the sidewalk. It was a major trauma for me. Our father decided to teach us a lesson in resourcefulness while attempting to retrieve my quarter. Without saying a word, he went into the local dime store and re-appeared with a long bamboo pole, and some chewing gum. He handed a stick of gum to each of us children and told us to chew it. While we chewed on our gum, our father proceeded to tell us a story of how precious money was when he was a child during the great depression. He and his brother gathered old pop bottles from trash cans so that they could go to a movie. Afterwards, he explained, they felt guilty that they had not taken the money home to help with groceries.

He then asked me to hand him my gum. After handing him my gum, he placed it on the end of the bamboo stick, and slick as you please, poked the stick through the grate and retrieved my shiny quarter!

This day always sticks in my mind. It was an example of how our parents, through their thoughts and actions, plus the very nature of the environment we lived in, added to the flavor of the times in which we children lived, seemed to teach us indelible lessons for the future. These lessons included resourcefulness, how to be independent thinkers, to have respect for other's thoughts and opinions, and to ask little, and what you will receive will always seem like so much more.

Chapter 24 - The North Fork of the Coeur d'Alene

Our father's mother and step-father lived on the North Fork of the Coeur d' Alene River. Imbedded in me, still, after all those years, are the sights, sounds and, most of all, scents of the ranch that lied at the edges of the North Fork not far from Cinnabar Creek, where they got their drinking water.

Memories hang like soft clouds of my father, uncle and grandfather cutting old cedar trees, with their fragrant scent, milling the logs, loading the boards. I see the sweat dripping off from under their felt hats, running down their sharp noses, the creases in their brows as they strained under a cross-cut saw. Sleeves rolled up as they work through the hot afternoon, shirts stripped off, down to white long-johns on the top, suspendered pants and heavy boots. I hear the sharp crack of trees as they find their resting place on the fern strewn forest floor. I turn toward the river and see the cows softly grazing on the flats underneath old cedar stumps, large enough for a miniature playhouse, blackened by the 1910 fire.

I feel the mossy round rocks of the river under my feet as I wade out into the crisp cool water. A fish tickles my feet. My brother skips rocks on the bank. A baby sister gurgles on a flannel blanket where my mother and grandmother are setting out a picnic lunch. Flies buzz by and I catch the sharp, but musky scent of cow pies wafting on the moist river air. I am in heaven.

I returned to the North Fork last summer. I stood at the gate of my Grandmother and Grandfather's ranch. It stood the same in many ways. Yet, it was changed too. The small two room cabin no longer stands. The huge rope swing, made of twelve foot poles where I learned to swing and grew to dangle my growing bare feet in the lazy summer dust has crumpled into the ground. Growing by the old cedar stumps on the river flats are young cedars, lush bushes and tall river grasses. I catch my breath as I see a large herd of elk grazing like fat cows. I turn and look to the north. I see heaven again. This is new type of heaven. Nature has won. Man and nature are in harmony.

Elk, Grazing on the North Fork of the Coeur d'Alene

Old Cedar Stumps Left from the Fire of 1910 on the North Fork. The 1910 fire burned approximately three million acres. It involved three states, western Montana, northern Idaho, and a small part of eastern Washington.

111

In the distance, you can see Little Guard Lookout, A U.S. Forest Service lookout on the North Fork of the Coeur d'Alene, River. It isn't active any more, but is rented out in summers for vacationers that would like some adventure.

Chapter 25 - A Meeting of Rivers

The North Fork and the South Fork of the Coeur d'Alene River join at Cataldo, Idaho. Cataldo, to me, is not only a joining of two rivers, but a start of many things. It is the start of the chain lakes, which drain, in turn, into Coeur d'Alene Lake, the headwaters of the Spokane River. It is also contains a start or beginning in Idaho history with the oldest standing building in Idaho, the Cataldo Mission. It was constructed in 1848.

I would recommend anyone visiting Idaho, to make the trip to the Cataldo Mission, twenty two miles east of Coeur d'Alene, just off Interstate 90. It is a visit you will not forget.

The Cataldo Mission

Chapter 26 - The Power of Nature

Cataldo, Idaho and the Cataldo "flats" of the 1950s and 1960s was a murky, gray-brown, low-lying flat bleached of color and life. Old cedar stumps, remnants of the 1910 fire and years of drifting smelter smoke from the Bunker Hill smelting plant in Kellogg, permanently marked this low lying back water mud flat of the Coeur d'Alene river where the south fork and the north fork converge.

Much of the "tailings", (heavy metals for the mines upstream, mixed with chemicals used to bleach the precious metals from the crushed rock), sewage from upstream towns flushed for decades down the river, and garbage that before the early 1970s was indiscriminately pitched into the river as it flowed by homes upstream, ridding the homeowner of the bother, or stench of their household leftovers, or the worry of unwanted paint, chemicals, glass, boards, complete with nails, old roofing, dead animals, whatever went into the south fork of the Coeur d'Alene river to wash downstream toward these 'flats'. The 'pit stop' if you may, was Cataldo, Idaho. Some of everything, (especially during the heavy spring runoff) washed, then, beyond this "pit stop" to the bottom of one of a string of beautiful lakes that lie downstream and beyond.

Just thinking about it, the chain of what passes on, I realize that a lot of my own DNA lies in the bottom of all that mud.

Beginning in the mid 1960s, with the push for a cleaner environment, started about the time of the "Highway Beautification Act" signed in October 1965 by President Lyndon B. Johnson, a national consciousness began to instill measures to clean up our man made messes. Back then, it was commonplace to throw whatever you didn't need...beer can, coke can, gum wrapper, whatever, out the car window. Fortunately, there weren't many fast food places yet in the valley before the mid 1970s.

The 'flats' sat stoic, a silent reminder for years after the start of the cleanup. Dark cedar stumps set in a backdrop of desolate mud flats void of vegetation pointed skyward as if in a silent plea for the return of those long lost days before mining and logging brought man to this lush valley to rape it of its resources and leave scars in return.

In the late 1960s, a freeway was cut through the valley. It runs across the center of these wetlands, (something that probably would not be possible with present day wetland laws). This actually turned out to be a blessing in disguise. It cut off some of the water flow to part of the area, added new soil to much of it, and encouraged planting of a hardy species of grasses and plant life that could survive in adverse soils.

The years went by; the Bunker Hill smelter was closed. Environmental education became a focus. People became more conscious of their actions when the environment was involved. Laws became tougher in this area.

Now, fifty years later, the same dead, desolate "flats" are alive and thriving with fish, frogs, moose, elk, deer, bear, otter, osprey, and other birds and wildlife too numerous to mention. Lilly pads float in the backwater marshes. Songbirds trill in the evening breeze. The sun sets to ducks nesting, frogs boasting under an awesomely brilliant canvas of color and light painted by nature. The old cedar stumps' wish has been fulfilled.

Cataldo is now alive with waterfowl

Moose at Cataldo

Blue Heron, Cataldo, Idaho

More Inhabitants of the Silver Valley, Idaho

Ode to the Crooked Bridge

Once straight, sturdy and strong she stood proud without a quiver,

She forged a trusty path across a steely gray river.

The crooked bridge was built from mill boilers, two, piled with rocks and,

Topped by planks, and railroad ties, was set upon the river bottom sand.

She stood strong against the floods and the winter snows,

Withstanding wind, rain, and frozen ice flows.

She carried the weight of untold tons,

Then, sighed with seven children's first driving runs.

She whispered to cougar, coyote, elk and deer,

While hugging children's feet when the edge got near.

She carried seven children to school and then back.

That bridge never lost a child or a pack.

As with the elderly, they lean with time.

The bridge too, became a strong, but crooked line.

Floods in '65 added to her lean,

When furniture and houses floated under her beams.

Follow the boards, don't look to the creek.

Watch out for holes, if you're scared, don't speak.

If you are faint of heart, then, beware!

That crooked bridge might give you a scare.   (Continued)

Still, with no malice or evil intent,

The bridge stood strong, yet with each year, bent.

But progress is bigger than one little bridge.

I-90 was coming, just over the ridge.

The wreckers, they took her, with a boom and a sway.

The crooked bridge was gone in less than a day.

EeKraemer

To the Crooked Bridge, South Fork of the Coeur d'Alene River

1953 – 1976

In Conclusion

The stories in this book are true to the best of my memory.

Nature and Mother Earth are great teachers. I am a believer that all life is a great circle of re-use, re-birth, and renewal. Some of the most important talents that all humans possess are imagination, ingenuity and invention. Honing these talents is the key to making mankind's wildest dreams possible.

It is also hoped that these stories will foster a deep appreciation for why the Silver Valley, and all of northern Idaho has a special place in the hearts of people who have chosen to live here or were fortunate enough by birthright, all of whom have become part of its history .

Names have been altered in this story to protect the privacy of family members. Exact location of the family home site has also been left as obscure in respect for the privacy of family members.

Acknowledgements

I would like to thank all of my family members for their unconditional support and encouragement during the writing of this book.

The Bridge in High Water

www.ingramcontent.com/pod-product-compliance
Lightning Source LLC
Chambersburg PA
CBHW060506280326
41933CB00014B/2879